T0211081

HEALTHCARE INFORMATION PRIVACY AND SECURITY

REGULATORY COMPLIANCE AND DATA SECURITY IN THE AGE OF ELECTRONIC HEALTH RECORDS

Bernard Peter Robichau

Apress·

Healthcare Information Privacy and Security: Regulatory Compliance and Data Security in the Age of Electronic Health Records

ISBN-13 (pbk): 978-1-4302-6676-1

ISBN-13 (electronic): 978-1-4302-6677-8

Publisher: Heinz Weinheimer
Acquisitions Editor: Jeff Olson
Developmental Editor: Robert Hutchinson
Editorial Board: Steve Anglin, Mark Beckner, Ewan Buckingham, Gary Cornell, Louise Corrigan,
    James DeWolf, Jonathan Gennick, Jonathan Hassell, Robert Hutchinson, Michelle Lowman,
    James Markham, Matthew Moodie, Jeff Olson, Jeffrey Pepper, Douglas Pundick,
    Ben Renow-Clarke, Dominic Shakeshaft, Gwenan Spearing, Matt Wade, Steve Weiss
Coordinating Editor: Rita Fernando
Copy Editor: Laura Poole
Compositor: SPi Global
Indexer: SPi Global
Cover Designer: Anna Ishchenko

Distributed to the book trade worldwide by Springer Science+Business Media New York, 233 Spring Street, 6th Floor, New York, NY 10013. Phone 1-800-SPRINGER, fax (201) 348-4505, e-mail orders-ny@springer-sbm.com, or visit www.springeronline.com. Apress Media, LLC is a California LLC and the sole member (owner) is Springer Science + Business Media Finance Inc (SSBM Finance Inc). SSBM Finance Inc is a Delaware corporation.

For information on translations, please e-mail rights@apress.com, or visit www.apress.com.

Apress and friends of ED books may be purchased in bulk for academic, corporate, or promotional use. eBook versions and licenses are also available for most titles. For more information, reference our Special Bulk Sales–eBook Licensing web page at www.apress.com/bulk-sales.

Any source code or other supplementary materials referenced by the author in this text is available to readers at www.apress.com. For detailed information about how to locate your book's source code, go to www.apress.com/source-code/.

Apress Business: The Unbiased Source of Business Information

Apress business books provide essential information and practical advice, each written for practitioners by recognized experts. Busy managers and professionals in all areas of the business world—and at all levels of technical sophistication—look to our books for the actionable ideas and tools they need to solve problems, update and enhance their professional skills, make their work lives easier, and capitalize on opportunity.

Whatever the topic on the business spectrum—entrepreneurship, finance, sales, marketing, management, regulation, information technology, among others—Apress has been praised for providing the objective information and unbiased advice you need to excel in your daily work life. Our authors have no axes to grind; they understand they have one job only—to deliver up-to-date, accurate information simply, concisely, and with deep insight that addresses the real needs of our readers.

It is increasingly hard to find information—whether in the news media, on the Internet, and now all too often in books—that is even-handed and has your best interests at heart. We therefore hope that you enjoy this book, which has been carefully crafted to meet our standards of quality and unbiased coverage.

We are always interested in your feedback or ideas for new titles. Perhaps you'd even like to write a book yourself. Whatever the case, reach out to us at editorial@apress.com and an editor will respond swiftly. Incidentally, at the back of this book, you will find a list of useful related titles. Please visit us at www.apress.com to sign up for newsletters and discounts on future purchases.

The Apress Business Team

For my dear wife, Christine, who is my constant motivation to strive toward integrity and honor, which is, in the end, the reason for this book.

Contents

Foreword ix

About the Author. xi

Acknowledgments xiii

Introduction xv

Chapter 1:   Introduction 1

Part I: The Evolution of a Monster. 7

Chapter 2:   Waking the Sleeping Giant. 9

Chapter 3:   It's Not Just HIPAA 21

**Part II: Divide and Conquer: Defining Ownership to
              Develop Solutions 31**

Chapter 4:   Assembling the Team. 33

Chapter 5:   Sifting through the Wreckage 43

Chapter 6:   Review Your Policies and Develop a Plan. 63

Part III: Sustainable Solutions 67

Chapter 7:   Identity and Access Management. 69

Chapter 8:   Application Design. 81

Chapter 9:   Access Validation Process 99

Chapter 10:   Physical and Environmental Safeguards 109

Chapter 11:   Systemwide and Client-Based Security. 117

Chapter 12:   Safeguarding Patient Data from Prying Eyes 123

**Part IV: From Project to Program: Transitioning to a
              Sustainable Support Model. 131**

Chapter 13:   People, the Most Crucial Element 133

Chapter 14:   Business Associates 137

Chapter 15:   Security Project versus Operational Support. 143

Chapter 16:   Putting the Plan in Place. 151

Part V: Appendices. 155

Appendix A: Sample Business Associate Agreement. 157

Appendix B: Sample Rules of Behavior for Privileged User Accounts. . 167

Appendix C: Breach Notification Process 171

Index 175

Foreword

Thoughts on Privacy and Security from a Medical Professional

For those of us who have been on the journey to create an electronic patient medical record, we first must recognize that we are still in our infancy. There is much work to do. Our goal is noble and achievable. We will create one patient record, which all caregivers use. It will be up to date, it will contain all "knowable" information about the patient, and it will be available to all at the point of care—be that the hospital ER, the doctor's office, an ER across the country, or the patient's home. But we must be ever mindful that in our effort to codify the information, we run the risk of losing the rich story of the patient.

Throughout my medical training as well as my 25 years of medical practice, I have been taught by my professors and patients that, if I listen carefully, the patient will tell me what is wrong with them. Yes, I will order some testing, but 90 percent of the time the patient will give me the diagnosis if I just listen to their *story*. My test serves to confirm what I already know to be true. How very precious and sacred is that story! It must be captured in the medical record so that the physicians and nurses who help us deliver the medical care are enlightened by the story.

What's this got to do with the book you have in your hands? Everything! The story will contain very personal and private information that deserves to be kept that way. Only those individuals who are caring for a particular patient should have the privilege of seeing her information.

What Peter Robichau has given you in this marvelous book is not only a great plan for the organization of your EMR security, but also a mindset to approach the data and its care. Follow its principles and your organization will sleep well at night. Ignore some steps, and your organization risks great peril and embarrassment, as well as financial punishment.

Peter points out the importance of regular self-audits as well as preparing for the "surprise letter" from the agency announcing an upcoming external audit. I could not agree more with this practice. In my hospital we refer to this as *systems assurance*—we know where the data is, who has access to it, how we grant them access, and we audit the process regularly to verify its integrity.

■ **Note** You really must plan for that audit. With all the *meaningful use* dollars the government has given out, do you really think they are going to sit back and see how this big experiment works? No, they will be demonstrating that they are clawing back as many of those billions of dollars as possible.

Read this book in its entirety. Yes, you will go back to review chapters as you work through your project, but you must have the framework and see the total picture to ensure you have it *right*.

Special emphasis needs to be placed on Chapter 13. As our information becomes more mobile—picture the doctor accessing patient information on her iPhone while at dinner—the importance of *"Training the Masses to Respect the System"* is crucial. For if you have done everything else right but have not educated your staff on how to keep the data private, you will have lost!

You will enjoy this book. It is well written and engagingly sprinkled with personal accounts that make it interesting.

My favorite politician, Sir Winston Churchill, is said to have said: "The Americans will get it right, but only after they have tried everything else." Don't be one of those who try everything else first. Follow the guidelines in the book; you will be glad you did.

Enjoy!

Michael Clore Sanders, M.D., F.A.A.F.P.
Chief Medical Information Officer
Flagler Hospital
Saint Augustine, Florida

About the Author

Bernard Peter Robichau is the owner and chief security consultant at Category 3 Partners, LLC, on contract with a large academic medical system in the mid-Atlantic. He is a Certified Professional in Health Information Management Systems, an Epic Certified Security Coordinator, and a Project Management Professional credential holder. He has nearly two decades of experience in the IT field with an emphasis on information security. Robichau has served as a security officer in the public sector and as a member on various information security advisory committees. He has presented on the topic of information security in public forums. For information related to this book, see its dedicated site at robichau.com.

Acknowledgments

Keith, who showed me how to lead well.

Charles, who taught me the importance of stepping up my game.

Jeanne, who cared when it mattered most and taught me to do the same.

Heather, who led with grace in the midst of many storms.

Allison, for showing me what great management looks like.

Michael and Maryanne, for always bringing integrity and excellence to the patient care process.

Martha, Justin, Jonathan, Judy, Mike, Chioma, Andrew, and *all* of the other analysts who raise the bar high.

Tim, for holding down the fort.

Paul and Gerald, for being simply brilliant and giving me something to strive toward.

Rick, Paul, Dane, Matt, and Phuong, for being the best team members ever.

Robert and Rita, for their exceeding patience and grace.

And finally, Mom, Stephan, Nadia, Marina, and Isaac, who are long-suffering and loving toward me always, even when I don't deserve it.

Introduction

This book is not about information security or healthcare information security in general. It is about electronic medical record (EMR) security—the difficult task of ensuring privacy and security in the evolving world of digitized patient data.

I receive so many urgent calls from people seeking assistance and guidance with their EMR security projects that I can't begin to respond to them all. That unmet need motivated me to write this book to impart the methods I have found to work most successfully. Most of it I wrote in hotel rooms and airport lounges during my constant travels as an EMR consultant. I am still amazed (though no longer surprised) when I find myself sitting next to someone in an airport using EMR software. The other day I found myself hammering out a chapter while involuntarily eavesdropping on one end of a conference call about an EMR project. It was as though the EMR buzzwords and project phases I was typing in our specialist space were mysteriously leaking into the public air!

Patient data is being transitioned from paper to electrons very rapidly, and the goal of EMR ubiquity is fast approaching. It is my hope that this book will help those who are struggling with the huge task of securing the EMR. It is a task that is important to me personally and one that should be given top priority in healthcare organizations everywhere because it is, quite simply, the right thing to do.

Introduction

The Long-Awaited Manual

There is no terror in the bang, only in the anticipation of it.

—Alfred Hitchcock

I was a veteran of the information technology world, and IT security had become my specialty—it was a domain I particularly enjoyed. I ventured into the healthcare space to work on a project that was driven largely by the HITECH Act (discussed in Chapter 2) and financial incentives related to the implementation and "meaningful use" of *electronic medical record* (EMR) systems.

Note An *electronic medical record* (EMR) is a system used by a provider to manage patient care. An *electronic health record* (EHR) is the set of patient data associated with an individual and spans multiple providers. An EHR is portable by nature, whereas an EMR is a system used by a provider or group of providers. "Meaningful use" is a term of art deployed by federal agencies to denote conformity to a set of explicit and measurable goals that inform EMR implementation to ensure capabilities such as physician order entry and online access by patients to their patient charts.

My job was to guide analysts through the process of building an application that facilitated efficient workflows while complying with organizational and regulatory standards of access.

I was given my marching orders, and I assembled an interdisciplinary team that would work over the course of the next 18 months to ensure that the application was deployed securely and appropriately to a user base that spanned all stakeholders from surgeons and nurses to environmental service workers and billing employees.

The objective was clear, and the markers for success were identifiable. I should have been on solid footing at the beginning of this project ... but I was not.

The Problem

What I soon discovered was that there were as many interpretations of the phrase "appropriate access" as there were stakeholders in the project. Moreover, there are significant legal (and therefore financial) implications associated with decisions surrounding application access. The patient data that lie at the core of an EMR system are highly sensitive, and any disclosure of these data due to negligence can lead to costly litigation and fines. The more basic but no less important issue I faced was the fiduciary responsibility to treat the customer's private information with the utmost care.

Professional Ethics

There is an inherent problem with EMR systems: They are built on the assumption that the consolidation of patient data for the purpose of broad, comprehensive access (by healthcare providers) will lead to better patient outcomes, lower costs, and a more efficient healthcare system. The problem is that this assumption about access is often at odds with the nature of the data being handled.

Note   *Access, availability,* and *privacy* are recurring themes throughout this book. The goal of the healthcare IT professional is to balance these three pillars of healthcare information privacy and security so that efficient care is facilitated while safeguarding private data.

In many cases, the analysts who design and implement access controls are safeguarding not only the confidential data of a generic customer but also their own health records—test results, diagnoses, and sensitive personal information.

Since the birth of modern medicine, we have been taught that our physicians are entitled to know about the most private aspects of our lives so that they can provide the most effective care to us. This is a level of confidentiality that is typically reserved for family members, clergy, and counselors. Healthcare professionals are morally and legally culpable if they ever handle patient data with reckless disregard for the patient's assumption and the law's requirement that all such data will be closely guarded and provided only to those with a demonstrated need to access it legitimately.

Vendor Guidance

A natural place to turn with a question about software is the application vendors. They provide the software deployed by the people charged with implementing and managing complex EMR systems, and it stands to reason that they will have the answers to tough questions.

Application vendors are, however, justifiably hesitant to provide detailed guidance in the realm of security and compliance. They prefer, instead, to facilitate the implementation of their software in alignment with the organization's policies and standards, which presumably address access, availability, and privacy.

What does this mean for the people charged with implementing and managing complex EMR systems?

1. Vendors will be valuable source of information about the options available and how other and often similar customers have done it.

2. Vendors will not offer definitive answers about what the customer should do.

3. Your organization will need to sift through the options and choose the best solution to your unique circumstances.

If your organization does not have mechanisms in place to consider all of the complex issues and make decisions regarding standards of access, there will be sustained disorder in your security and compliance program. This is why it is so important to establish the ground rules and processes that will lead to a consistently built and secure EMR system.

Many Hats

Going into that first EMR project, I had assumed that my thorough knowledge of information security regulations, practices, and technologies would be adequate for the task at hand. I did not realize that my job would require me to be simultaneously a technologist, diviner, and mediator—all in an effort to bring together the complex worlds of access, regulatory compliance, and usability. Recognizing that many different skills are required to achieve success is often the first step in this long journey. It is quite possible to "herd cats" to ensure your users' access to everything they need and your customers' data security.

The Audience

I thought many times during various EMR projects that a guide or manual of some sort would be a godsend. It is my hope that what follows will help bridge the gaps between all of the disparate, often competing interests that accompany the implementation and management of an EMR system. The medical field certainly needs to push ahead with the implementation of new technologies—but not at the expense of privacy and security.

Note How you use this book will differ depending on your role in the privacy and security life cycle. Although some of the more technical chapters might seem irrelevant to managers or directors, do not be fooled! Perhaps a very careful reading of these chapters will not be required by all, but it is important that managers and directors understand what is at stake so that the technical staff can be held accountable for addressing these critical areas.

Who will benefit from this book? First, it is important to understand that this is not a technical manual to aid in each iteration of the project (though it will certainly assist in this regard). Rather, this is a technical book for business operations. It will help each stakeholder understand the issues at hand and the technologies or solutions that can help in achieving organizational goals. These include but are not limited to:

- **Executives:** Those who serve as project sponsors will do well to understand the competing interests surrounding privacy and security.

- **IT directors and managers:** There are enough topics related to the management of people who manage systems to make this book a resource for department directors, office managers, and others with an interest in how organizational goals are being implemented.

- **Technical staff and analysts:** It should not be assumed that the application analyst is the only member of the technical staff who needs to know the ins and outs of EMR privacy and security. System administrators, database administrators (DBAs), and help desk staff all need to understand what is at stake.

- **Information security officers and staff:** It might seem obvious that your information security personnel would need to understand the issues surrounding EMR security, but old staffing models—whereby security personnel managed antivirus definitions, virtual private networks (VPNs), and firewalls simply don't account for EMR access issues. Your chief information security officer (CISO), security architects, administrators, and provisioning staff will benefit from an understanding of the EMR security.

- **Ancillary compliance offices:** Your health information management (HIM), corporate compliance, and legal staff will benefit from this manual as much as your technical staff will.

- **EMR vendors:** Employees of EMR vendors often have a non- healthcare background (many having entered the field straight out of college) and will benefit from a thorough understanding of privacy and security issues.

- **Consultants:** The outside people who are often brought in to assist with project or program management will need a good foundation in healthcare information privacy and security.

The Goal

Whether your EMR system is pre-, mid-, or post-implementation, your goals are the same: a system built with privacy and security integrated throughout, and a security program that facilitates a continued focus on the same.

- If you are **pre-implementation**, congratulations! You are starting out with a tool chest of information that will help ensure that you build your system, and develop your processes properly.

- If you are **mid-implementation**, struggling to align the competing interests within your organization as you build your EMR system, then you will have the reinforcements you need to get back on track and finish with a huge success.

- If you are **post-implementation**, and struggling with some of the basic concepts addressed in this book, you should be able to tackle each domain related to privacy and security, refine (or redesign if necessary) your existing privacy and security program.

The end result in each case is a sustainable security program that allows the organization to assure its customers that their data is treated with the care that they should expect from any reputable healthcare office or system. A trustworthy security program is not an option in the field of HIM but an obligation. In a world where personal data is proliferating at an exponential rate, it must be properly safeguarded lest it fall into the wrong hands.

You have your marching orders, and you are about to acquire the tools you need to carry them out!

The Evolution of a Monster

Waking the Sleeping Giant

A Brief History of Healthcare IT

I fear all we have done is to awaken a sleeping giant and fill him with a terrible resolve.

—Admiral Isoroku Yamamoto, *Tora! Tora! Tora!*

It was 1996, and I had my first job in the IT world. The floppy disk drives I knew in my youth were disappearing, desktop productivity tools were powerful and easy to use, and the World Wide Web was making its way into households across the world.

The Problem with Paper

One thing I noticed soon after arriving at my new job was a process for data sharing that was problematic.

Every morning at about 10 o'clock, an employee in the communications office would emerge in the copy room with a pile of hand-snipped news clippings, which would be assembled and photocopied to form a thick stack of news that was relevant to the industry in which we worked.

This bundle of trade news was then reproduced countless times, stapled, and delivered by the mailroom to division directors and executives for mid-day perusing.

I watched this well-paid middle manager repeat this process each day, using his expert judgment to determine what news was important to share with his colleagues. I even saw this important job handed off to another manager when the original "news clipper" retired.

This stood in stark contrast to the growing number of newspaper websites that shared the same type of information directly with consumers on their Internet-connected computers. I remember looking on with amazement the first time I saw the *USA Today* website slowly render across a computer screen over a dial-up connection several years earlier and wondered just where this new technology was going to take us.

In short order, the venerable tradition of clipping trade articles, photocopying them, and disseminating the packets of information fell by the wayside. It had become obvious that paper was an inefficient way to share information, and businesses were adapting as a result.

By 1998, I had several years of IT experience under my belt. The Internet was proving itself as a productivity tool, and the personal computer was becoming ubiquitous—no longer a toy of hobbyists and geeks. The place to be was telecom or any field related to Internet technologies.

Systems were growing faster, and the demand for new technologies that leveraged ever-increasing bandwidth, which allowed data to flow at greater speeds, was huge. Moore's law was in effect, and any doubt that we were living in the Information Age was laid to rest.[1]

For the next three years I gobbled up the expanding crop of new data-driven technologies. I learned about data packets and the protocols in which they traveled, and I was amazed at how digital content was being used and leveraged to change the way we think and how we do business.

The Downside of Connectivity

Along with my newfound obsession with all things data, I became acutely aware of the inherent dangers of a connected, data-driven digital age. Gone were the days of isolated networks of terminals connected to mainframes that housed an organization's critical data. As PCs were connected to servers and both were connected to the Internet, it became critical to ensure that the data on those servers (and PCs) was carefully guarded from the growing threat of hackers and Internet thieves.

---

[1]Moore's law is the empirical induction that gains in technology double every two years, allowing for dramatic increases in computing trends from year to year.

Data became the commodity-driving business and, as the currency of the digital age, it was a prime target for theft and sabotage.

It was like a game of cloak-and-dagger: implementing firewalls to protect assets, reviewing logs, adjusting rules for the transmission of data, and trying to stay one step ahead of the "bad guys."

Elsewhere in America ...

While the rest of the world scrambled to ensure a smooth transition from paper business transactions to digital commerce and do so securely, the healthcare industry plodded along its course, and the paper chart remained the primary means of reviewing and documenting patient care.

Physician practices and hospitals adopted computerized billing and scheduling systems, in many cases long before the proliferation of the Internet. But patient data—the most important digital asset of the healthcare industry—continued to reside on paper.

Businesses ventured into the digital frontier, finding new ways to use computing power to change the way business was done, but healthcare systems maintained the status quo. The paper chart, made from good old-fashioned milled tree pulp, sat stubbornly at the core of the healthcare business model.

The End Result

Since technology was at best an afterthought in the healthcare world, budgets reflected a lack of commitment to information technologies, and top IT talent did not seek out physician practices and health systems when looking for work.

This lack of innovation created a brain drain in the healthcare IT space at a time when the rest of the business world was finding new ways to drive business through IT. When systems such as e-mail and file management were introduced in healthcare, they often remained static and weren't upgraded as new features were introduced.

Old technologies and aging systems were often propped up to keep them running, and they were not replaced when they should have been. IT was not at the core of the enterprise, because it provided only peripheral value to the organization. Instead of being integrated into the business model, the IT department was often viewed by healthcare executives on the same level as the mailroom or facilities management—necessary, but not critical.

Perhaps a healthcare IT job provided a reliable paycheck for some, but it certainly wasn't a space where the brightest could be challenged and grow. Paper was king, and the healthcare world was fine with this model.

The Problem

Think back to the news clipper, beavering away with a newspaper, a pair of scissors, and a photocopier each day, doing his best to ensure that important information made its way into the hands of the people who needed it.

Few would argue that his task was unimportant—managers and executives certainly need to keep abreast of news and trends in their industries. The issue was this: when information can be digitized, as with the newspaper, sharing it via paper becomes inefficient.

Another problem with paper-based information sharing is the method of aggregating the data. In the case of the news clipper, he was the arbiter of what was important and what was not. In this analog newspaper world, the process of information sharing goes something like this:

1. The newspaper editors determine what is newsworthy and what is not.

2. Stories are written, proofed, edited, and compiled for publication on a daily basis.

3. The paper is printed and assembled.

4. The paper is delivered.

5. The news clipper reads through the paper, making a judgment call as to what is important and what is not.

6. The articles deemed important (by the news clipper) are extracted, collated, and assembled into an information packet.

7. The packets are distributed to management.

8. Managers read through the information packets with an eye for items of relevance to them.

Notice several things about this process:

- The extremely linear system makes it probable that the data will get to management too late. News that arrives in this analog format is likely to become stale quickly.

- Managers are likely to miss articles that are important to them, but were deemed unimportant by the news aggregator, the news clipper.

- An analog process is used when a more efficient, digital process could be employed.

Certainly, there are some stories provided by newspapers that are not time-sensitive, and there is something to be said for the tactile and sensory experience of picking up a freshly printed newspaper and reading it over a cup of coffee. There is nothing I like more than to read the Sunday issue of the *New York Times* front to back, but I don't read it to keep up with breaking news. The *New York Times* has, in turn, refocused on in-depth features and human interest stories, keeping their medium viable in this digital age—but they are still struggling to compete in this world of bits and bytes.

It's a different ball game now, and an attempt to preserve old processes for the sake of nostalgia or familiarity will lead to obsolescence and obscurity—not a worthy goal in any case.

The Healthcare Industry Analog

The goal of a paperless society has proven unrealistic, at least in the short term. By many accounts, indeed, our digital age has *increased* reliance on paper, because we have taken the abundance of new data of all sorts as a call to print even more than ever. Nonetheless, paper transactions have been disappearing steadily as digital transactions replace them.

Think about the financial industry, where withdrawing cash from the bank once required writing out a paper check to "Cash" in front of a human bank teller. Now, an ATM dispenses the same cash, with no face-to-face human involvement, and the customer has the option of taking a paper receipt or declining it.

The obsession with paper in the healthcare world did not subside as it did in other sectors of the business world. Let's look at the (once) common work-flow in a physician's office during a patient encounter:

1. The patient arrives for a visit, and the physician makes a general inquiry about the reason for the visit.

2. The patient presents his current state and describes his symptoms as thoroughly as possible.

3. The physician proceeds through an exchange about the symptoms with the patient, which might involve taking notes or might be purely verbal.

4. The physician plans a course of treatment, conveys this to the patient, and documents what transpired in the patient's paper chart.

5. The physician might make a referral on paper to a specialist.

6. The patient arrives at the specialist either with or without a copy of his paper chart, and the specialist asks the same questions the physician had asked on the previous visit.

7. The specialist plans a course of treatment, and the notes about this encounter were placed in yet another paper chart housed at the specialist's office.

In this scenario, the provider should probably follow some better practices, but there is nothing about this paper-based process that facilitates an efficient workflow.

- Perhaps the provider began by reviewing current medications with the patient (always a good place to begin an office visit), or perhaps, being pressed for time, he began addressing symptoms.

- If the primary encounter happened to be documented thoroughly, there would be a fairly high chance that the visit notes would be only partially legible to anyone other than the primary provider.

- In the event of a referral, the original paper chart and all of the valuable data it contains are likely to remain at the primary care provider's office because it is cumbersome to transfer. The specialist will often be starting from scratch.

- Additionally, information such as blood pressure, heart rate, test results, and so on would have resided within the "commotion" of the physician notes, and a correlation of these critical numbers from a series of visits would have been difficult and time-consuming.

There are so many uncontrollable variables introduced by the paper chart that inefficiency is the least of our concerns. Patient care begins to suffer when health data is maintained in multiple places in a linear fashion.

Just as patient care can suffer when all aspects of care are documented on paper, huge gains in patient care can be achieved when best practices are enforced by computer systems and discrete data is maintained in a manner that helps in diagnosis and trending.

Note Among other benefits, the fact that an *electronic medical record* (EMR) stores discrete data allows the key metrics related to the health of a patient to be analyzed and acted on. For instance, when key lab results are maintained as separate fields in a database that can be compared over time, software can find trends that might go unnoticed by a provider, triggering a different approach to patient care.

A Movement Afoot

Even though providers were devoted to the paper chart, it was inevitable that some in the medical field would recognize the potential of technology to benefit patient care. While the giants such as Xerox, Digital Equipment Corporation, and IBM were well on their way to revolutionizing the business world with information technology (IT), a revolutionary idea was brewing in the mind of a recent MIT graduate.

In the 1960s, Neil Pappalardo, a young physics student, was struggling to write his senior thesis when it was suggested that he collaborate with some cardiologists who needed some help. The result was a medical device that examined the electrical signal from a patient's heart. Pappalardo's project was a success, his thesis topic was determined, and his major changed from physics to electrical engineering.

This foray into the medical field led Pappalardo to a job in the computer science lab at Mass General Hospital, where he began to write software to automate the hospital's clinical laboratory and other areas.

Because his position was funded by the National Institutes of Health, his work product was in the public domain. So, in 1968 the programming language MUMPS (Massachusetts General Hospital Utility Multi-Programming System) was created, and the following year Pappalardo founded a company called Meditech (Medical Information Technology) to leverage MUMPS to automate healthcare processes.

The story of Pappalardo and Meditech is perhaps unremarkable. Similar stories can be told about other visionaries and the founding of other companies in any field. But the stage was set, and the healthcare IT world boomed in the following decades to include companies such as General Electric (formerly IDX and Centricity), Cerner, Allscripts, and Epic.

As previously noted, these new trends in healthcare IT did not revolutionize patient care when IT was revolutionizing the rest of the world around us. For the longest time, advances in healthcare IT remained largely confined to business processes (such as scheduling) and order entry (such as prescribing).

What is remarkable about Pappalardo's story is the fact that MUMPS acted as the foundation of many systems that eventually drove the EMR race.

Catching MUMPS

In 1976, eight years after MUMPS was released into the public domain, a graduate student at the University of Wisconsin named Judy Faulkner started developing a program to manage patient information.

Faulkner turned to MUMPS as the foundation of her efforts, and when the resulting program was a success, she began to sell it to hospitals and community health centers.

■ **Note**   MUMPS, along with the Cache database from InterSystems, acts as the foundation for Epic's EMR as well as others. These might be unfamiliar products to the IT professional who doesn't work in healthcare, but they are essential technologies to understand if you are working with any of the EMR vendors who leverage these notably older technologies.

What followed was the founding of a company called Human Services Computing, which is now Epic Systems. Fast-forward almost 40 years, and Epic Systems now boasts that more than 50 percent of the US population has its health information stored in an Epic digital record.

The Intervening Years

What transpired in the years after the seminal creations by Pappalardo and Faulkner was the creation of a host of systems that introduced technology into medical practice—each with varying degrees of success. There have been leaders in the field, but there was no analog in the healthcare IT space to the Apple versus Microsoft rivalry.

There have been leaders in the field of scheduling and leaders in the field of e-prescribing. Some vendors excelled in the world of ambulatory practice management, and some were the best at order entry. What these niche vendors did from 1970 to 2000 was to highlight the importance of technology in facilitating the complex workflows involved in patient care.

A Voice from Above

With all of the buzz today about the *Affordable Care Act* (ACA a.k.a. Obamacare), *meaningful use*, and the like, people have come to equate federal initiatives related to the adoption of EMR systems with the administration of President Barack Obama.

It was, however, President George W. Bush who created the Office of National Coordinator (ONC) for Healthcare Information Technology within the office of the US Department of Health and Human Services (HHS) in 2004 to coordinate the use of healthcare IT and the electronic exchange of health information.

▨ **Note**   You will need to become familiar with news, rulings, and statements from the National Coordinator—the appointed head of the ONC. As standards change or regulations are adjusted in regard to healthcare IT, they are coordinated and communicated through the ONC. For more information, see healthit.gov/buzz-blog.

Bush, or perhaps his advisors, saw the compelling need to advance the adoption and use of technology to improve patient care. This was also the first step in the process of controlling spiraling costs triggered by duplicated efforts and fragmented care plans.

The Financial Crisis and the EMR Rush

Just three years after the establishment of the ONC, the world found itself in the midst of financial troubles unlike anything seen since the Great Depression. By 2008 the financial troubles were officially labeled a crisis when the markets plunged and major financial institutions faced the very real possibility of collapse.

To prevent a worldwide financial depression, the US government turned to a series of financial stimulus packages. Troubled assets were purchased by central banks and a series of economic stimulus packages were passed by Congress, the most significant of which was the American Recovery and Reinvestment Act (ARRA) of 2009. Perhaps you have seen the name of this legislative act on signs next to highway construction projects funded by ARRA.

The ARRA legislation included a provision specific to healthcare IT dubbed the *Health Information Technology for Economic and Clinical Health Act* (HITECH Act).

▨ **Note**   The HITECH Act is a critical piece of legislation that it is critical for you to know inside and out, because it clarifies in detail the legal and legislative guidelines related to healthcare information privacy and security. Read more about it online at http://www.healthit.gov/ policy-researchers-implementers/hitech-act-0.

The HITECH Act was nothing less than a sweeping piece of legislation that was intended to hasten the adoption of EMR systems by providing incentives for the *meaningful* implementation of certified EMRs.

What scores of vendors had sought to promote in isolation for decades—the digitization of critical patient data—was now incentivized by the promise of large government payouts. Questions related to how certain tasks should be accomplished within the EMR were answered by the HITECH Act. If providers and organizations wanted a piece of the nearly $20 billion that was set aside to encourage meaningful EMR implementations, they were obliged to follow the rules laid out in the HITECH Act.

Think about the Possibilities

It is only logical. The financial world was in turmoil and credit had seized up; pumping life into the economy through the healthcare sector, which accounted for almost 20 percent of gross domestic product (GDP) in the United States at this point, was a surefire way to help revive a failing economy.

But the opportunistic legislators in our nation's capital were not primarily concerned with economic health. Although the HITECH Act is clearly concerned with economic health, we need to parse out the phrase "economic and clinical health" in the legislation's title to understand what is at stake.

Let's go back to the figure cited above—the fact that healthcare accounts for almost 20 percent of GDP in the United States. Although this number is actually closer to 17 percent, the figure is staggering and is the highest national percentage of spending on healthcare in the world. Though the United States has, by certain measures of certain portions of its population, the best quality healthcare in the world, its healthcare spending continues to spiral out of control and out of proportion to outcomes. With government programs such as Medicare and Medicaid footing the bill for ever-increasing quantity and cost of visits and procedures, there is a huge incentive to control costs.

It is still possible to provide decent care to a single patient without a digital health record. From the moment he walks in the door of a doctor's office through surgery and postoperative care, a patient with a paper chart can expect good treatment in the United States (though there are certainly efficiencies to be gained through the use of computerized systems).

The huge potential cost savings from the use of digital health records comes through *population health management*. We can speak about the consumer benefits provided by *electronic health records* (EHRs)—and online access to personal health records is mandated in the HITECH Act—but these benefits are peripheral to the primary goal of the EMR.

When information in a patient chart is segmented into *discrete data*, the possibilities for improving patient care and decreasing costs are endless.

Consider the most basic information in a patient chart: the patient's date of birth. This information alone can trigger an automatic appointment for prostate exams or mammograms that might otherwise be overlooked until a costly and perhaps lethal diagnosis is made later in life.

The paper chart helps doctors understand the patients sitting in front of them. The EMR, on the other hand, helps the organization recognize who is not coming in for a visit that should be.

On a macro level, the data collected in lab draws and even vitals collected over time can help statisticians correlate trends in pathologies and diseases, leading to better preventive care in the future. Perhaps the data collected on you today won't keep you healthier now, but when combined with the data of millions of other patients, it might save thousands of lives a decade from now.

Cost-effective population health management is the ultimate aim of the EMR initiative. With the establishment of the ONC and the enactment of the HITECH Act, we are on our way to realizing the dream if the tools at our disposal are used wisely.

Pandora's Box

With all of that new personal health data in databases across the country, the ONC realized that the risk of privacy violation and identity theft was much higher.

The federal government had previously imposed some guidelines regarding expectations of privacy related to patient data in the *Health Insurance Portability and Accountability Act of 1996* (HIPAA), but most industry officials would tell you that many practitioners were lax in following these rules and the government was lax in enforcing them.

The HITECH Act put teeth in the enforcement of existing HIPAA rules and extended regulations related to:

- *Breach notification*: specifically related to the disclosure of unencrypted patient data (generally of more than 500 patient records).

- *ePHI access*: accommodating digital access to the patient's *protected health information* (PHI) and chart by the patient for a nominal fee and in short order.

- *Business associate regulation*: no longer can organizations turn a blind eye to their business partners. They are required to require that business partners conform to the same standards of privacy and security as their own employees.

- *Willful neglect*: acts of willful neglect that lead to disclosures, or unauthorized access, of PHI will be subject to fines and penalties.

The Stage Is Set

The years of the Great Recession that followed the 2008 financial meltdown coincided with the years of the implementation of the HITECH Act, which propelled the rapid and concerted adoption of EMR systems across the United States. Patient data began to flow into these systems at a staggering rate, and the job of securing this data, ensuring that it was used properly, and didn't fall into the wrong hands was often an afterthought.

As EMR systems begin to do their jobs and hospitals and physician practices settle into operational support mode, key employees must take a hard look at how the data they keep is being used and what they are doing to ensure that they are acting as trustworthy guardians of a very sensitive resource.

Further Reading

"MIT Alumni & Friends Profile: A. Neal & Jane Pappalardo, Pappalardo Fellowships," at http://web.mit.edu/physics/giving/profiles/pappalardo.html (accessed December 31, 2013).

"Meditech Corporate Timeline," at https://www.meditech.com/corporatetimeline/homepage.htm (accessed December 31, 2013).

Moukheiber, Zina, "Epic Systems' Tough Billionaire," Forbes.com, April 18, 2012, at http://www.forbes.com/sites/zinamoukheiber/2012/04/18/epic-systems-tough-billionaire/ (accessed December 31, 2013).

"About ONC," at http://www.healthit.gov/newsroom/about-onc (accessed December 31, 2013).

"Index for Excerpts from the American Recovery and Reinvestment Act of 2009 (ARRA)," at http://www.healthit.gov/sites/default/files/hitech_act_excerpt_from_arra_with_index.pdf.

Davidson, Kavitha, "The Most Efficient Healthcare Systems in the World," *Huffington Post*, August 29, 2013, at http://www.huffingtonpost.com/2013/08/29/most-efficient-healthcare_n_3825477.html (accessed December 31, 2013).

It's Not Just HIPAA

Legislating Privacy and Security

Laws control the lesser man. Right conduct controls the greater one.

—proverb

I remember the first time I signed a HIPAA privacy notice before a routine checkup. It was a rather lengthy form, and the practitioner wasn't terribly interested in having me read the whole thing but was rather insistent that I "initial here" and "sign there" so that the paper could be filed away, I assumed, in case there was some sort of a lawsuit involving the disclosure of my personal information.

In fact, what I had signed was not the medical equivalent of a liability waiver like the ones that I had signed before venturing out on Jet Ski excursions or parasailing adventures. Rather, it was a standard notice describing:

- That the covered entity (in this case, my family doctor) was permitted to use my protected health information for limited purposes and was required to get my permission to use it otherwise.

- That the covered entity was responsible for protecting my privacy.

- My privacy rights, and what I could do if I thought my rights had been violated.

- How to contact the covered entity for more information and to make a complaint.

The *Health Insurance Portability and Accountability Act of 1996* (HIPAA) was crafted primarily to address the growing problems of health insurance cancellations (hence the "portability" provisions of the act), but it also addressed the growing concerns about patient privacy (the "accountability" portion).

For many years, the enforcement of the privacy laws included in HIPAA were confined to checks on whether covered entities, as they were called—which included physician practices, health insurers, hospitals, and other businesses and organizations that regularly handled or processed sensitive patient data— were notifying their customers of their rights to privacy and confidentiality. Businesses knew that HIPAA didn't have a strong enforcement mechanism, and the federal government certainly didn't have the manpower to police the healthcare industry.

Minimum Necessary

A key protection within HIPAA was the license granted the covered entity to transmit *protected health information* (PHI) to the *minimum* extent *necessary* to facilitate medical treatment and billing, freeing practitioners from liability concerns that might otherwise arise in the process of conducting daily operations.

Countervailing limits were placed on the *release of protected information*— or more commonly just *release of information* (ROI)—by the covered entity. Patients had the right to expect that the type of information disclosed in the course of business was relevant to the transaction being processed. Therefore, a nurse would have no business seeing delinquent bills, and a biller would have no business seeing sensitive diagnoses. All of these expectations were clearly outlined in HIPAA.

Note   Keep this concept of the *minimum necessary* in mind as you read through the remaining chapters. We return to this standard several times, especially in Chapter 8.

HIPAA did not specify how the covered entities should accomplish these privacy measures but simply stated that this was the standard that should be followed.

More Accountability

In addition to the added layers of privacy that a patient should be able to expect, the covered entities were expected to document their privacy practices and appoint an individual who would be charged with overseeing security, compliance, and privacy oversight and enforcement.

For many small operations, this duty fell to the operations manager, who simply donned the "privacy officer" hat, but in larger organizations with complex operations, this was a daunting task.

Perhaps someone was in charge of information security (think *firewalls* and *antivirus*) while other people were in charge of corporate compliance. This new world blended the worlds of technology and compliance, and it was uncharted territory.

Think about the areas affected by patient privacy. You have many layers of operational staff handling sensitive patient data. You also have administrative staff, such as secretaries and IT professionals, with access to sensitive information. Environmental services employees and patient transport staff are all exposed to certain levels of private information, and these employees have to be trained and monitored. Patient data is copied and kept on hard drives, on paper, on desks, in databases, in file cabinets, or perhaps on removable digital media. How does the organization ensure that the flow of data is controlled and limited to the proper channels? How does the organization handle inappropriate disclosures of data? What's more, how does the organization correct the process that led to the inappropriate disclosure in the first place?

Security Rules

HIPAA was enacted in 1996, but various portions of the law were phased into place over time to give organizations a chance to come into compliance with new standards and expectations.

A key aspect of HIPAA is Part II, called the *Security Standards*, which are broken into three logical groupings: *Administrative Safeguards*, *Physical Safeguards*, and *Technical Safeguards*.

■ **Note** Whether you work in the field of corporate compliance, privacy, information technology, health information management, nursing informatics, or a related field, it is important to understand the security rules. The technical rules will apply more to some, and the administrative rules to others, but there are few positions in healthcare IT that will not be concerned (at all) with HIPAA security rules.

The Security Standards specify how the Department of Health and Human Services (HHS) expects each covered entity to ensure privacy and security in regard to protected health information.

Administrative Safeguards

The Administrative Safeguards in HIPAA are intended to force the organization to methodically account for its privacy and security practices. With the final ruling effective in 2003, organizations are legally obliged to have integrated privacy and security in their business practices. Handing out a HIPAA notice to patients annually is not compliance with the ruling!

What application of administrative safeguards looks like differs from organization to organization. The content of the HIPAA rule is more than 50 percent administrative, yet there aren't detailed instructions on how to apply these standards.

What is clear is that existing practices must be evaluated (*audited*), and deficiencies so identified must be addressed.

Some of the Administrative Safeguards that covered entities must address are:

- *Policies and procedures*: These must be documented, and the process of adopting them must be discernible. For example, who approved the policies, and how do they fit in with the compliance framework?

- *Accountability*: The buck has to stop with someone in the organization, and whether this person is called a *privacy officer*, a *chief security officer*, or another title, internal policies must reference that authority in matters of privacy.

- *Access controls*: How does the organization decide who is allowed to access what PHI? What is the process for creating accounts, elevating privileges, and terminating access?

- *Auditing*: How does the organization audit its security and privacy practices and correct for noncompliance? What is the frequency of internal audits, and who performs these? What are your audit processes?

Notice that these safeguards are open to interpretation, but the key factor here is the establishment of standards and subsequent record keeping. If you can't prove that you have complied with these standards, then in the eyes of the law, they simply aren't being followed (even if you are).

Physical Safeguards

Just as the administrative safeguards aim to ensure that an organization weaves privacy and security into its business processes, the physical security rules in HIPAA address the need to ensure that the physical environment where PHI is stored and rendered does not promote the unnecessary sharing of private information. Therefore, covered entities must consider:

- If adequate physical controls (badge-protected doors or physical security guards) protect areas where computer systems reside.

- Whether workstations are protected from unauthorized users, or the general public, by physical/visual barriers.

- How to ensure that PHI is guarded as equipment is introduced to the network and retired from operations. When it discarded, what is the organization's policy for ensuring that all PHI is removed?

The physical security of computers might seem like a no-brainer, but I am always amazed at the new and creative excuses that end users propose as reasons they cannot be bothered with a password or a reasonable timeout period on their system. The HIPAA ruling provides a very clear answer to those who cannot be bothered with the most basic measures that must be in place to ensure the integrity of patient data.

Technical Safeguards

HIPAA is, as noted, almost entirely administrative—mandating that we take care of patient data with good, solid practices in the enterprise. However, there is a certain amount of cybersecurity that must be employed to work with our best practices, ensuring the integrity of PHI.

Technical safeguards, according to HIPAA, should ensure:

- *Data integrity*: An organization is responsible for ensuring that the data in its care remains in an unaltered state. To use a technical term, *checksums* should validate that data is as we expect it to be. We should be able to trust that the blood pressure reading associated with Martha Smith is indeed hers and that her Social Security number is accurate. If we can't be sure that our data is accurate, then we have a problem.

- *Data protection*: The data housed in an enterprise should be safe. It should be encrypted when possible. It should be behind firewalls. It should be safe from viruses and hackers, and the customer should have every reason to believe that it will remain safely in the care of the organization.

- *Configuration management*: To avoid the inadvertent introduction of a change into the system that could lead to productivity or, worse, patient safety issues, the organization is responsible for maintaining a thorough record of configurations pertinent to its patient data systems.

- *Authentication*: How does the organization confirm that the person who is accessing your data is who he or she claims to be? The most basic level of authentication is a user id and password, but some organizations would do well to add a second layer of authentication, force password changes, add complexity to password requirements, and more. These are all aspects of the authentication requirement in HIPAA.

The HIPAA rule, in this case, extends from your administrative staff to the technical staff, and you can see how important it is to make sure that managers work with technical staff to implement and then document how they have complied with HIPAA.

The HIPAA privacy rule set the healthcare privacy and security machine in motion. Target dates were set, and there was an expectation that organizations would begin complying with the regulations that were established. But, as noted, there wasn't a great enforcement mechanism, and this was a problem.

HITECH Security

Chapter 2 touched on the fact that the HITECH Act of 2009 probably did more to encourage the digitization of health data and the adoption of electronic medical record (EMR) systems than the previous four decades of corporate marketing combined. What I did not cover there was the expansion of privacy and security regulations under the provisions of that law.

HIPAA was a valiant effort to raise awareness of the need to protect patient data, but it was just phase one. Those industry officials who were pushing for legislation that would encourage the adoption of EMR systems were also aware of the inherent privacy issues at stake. When you digitize patient data and make it more accessible to those providing care (or using the data for analytics), it can easily fall into the hands of people with nefarious intentions.

Identity thieves and snooping family members alike would love to see the contents of a patient chart, and it would require additional work to ensure that our increasingly connected health systems were increasingly secure and private. The old way of doing business would not be adequate as the healthcare world moved into the twenty-first century, and the architects of the HITECH Act knew that added attention to privacy and security had to be part of the legislation that would push more patient data online.

So the HITECH Act simultaneously guarantees greater patient rights and protections in regard to privacy and security while significantly increasing the potential liability of covered entities if they fail to comply with the regulations.

The beefing up of HIPAA regulations doesn't stop there; the HITECH Act grants HHS broader powers of enforcement against noncompliant providers and covered entities. The HITECH Act was a warning shot across the bow of the healthcare industry, which was, until 2009, operating under the assumption that since the risk of enforcement was low, there was little need to allocate resources to the complex and often expensive arena of privacy and security.

Note *Risk management* is a discipline in the business world that calculates the financial risk of many scenarios and determines the best path for an organization among the multiple options. A low-risk and low-cost scenario will almost always be selected over the low-risk and high-cost scenario, even when the latter is what needs to be done as a matter of integrity, privacy, and security. "What is the likelihood?" executives will ask. The fashioners of the HITECH Act aimed to increase the risk to covered entities from poor privacy practices and thereby incentivize their adherence to the law.

The HITECH legislation specifically singled out the all-too-common practice of "willful neglect," where a covered entity knowingly permitted bad practices, system misuse, security risks, and flagrant disregard for the integrity of PHI. Health systems that might have turned a blind eye to privacy and security in the past will certainly pay attention to fines that can soar to well over $1 million for repeat offenders.

Further delineated in the HITECH Act are standards for breach notification. If a covered entity "loses" data related to, generally, more than 500 patients, standard notification processes kick into gear. The public must be notified of such breaches, and the details of the breach are posted publically on a wall of shame (of sorts) maintained by HHS. This negative deterrent was reinforced by requiring local media to be notified when certain criteria of a breach were met.

Misplace a laptop with spreadsheets full of patient data? Data breach! Depending on the number of records on the laptop, a simple slip-up like this could be a media nightmare for an organization, costing business and the trust of the patient population they serve.

While HIPAA laid down the law about what needed to be done, the HITECH Act was HHS's way of saying, "And we mean it!"

The Omnibus Rule of 2013

A quick note is required regarding what many refer to as the *Omnibus Rule of 2013*.

When it came to *business partners*—those business associates that a healthcare organization might contract with but did not manage directly—there was a convenient document called the *business partner agreement* (BPA) that healthcare organizations loved.

Note   Business Partner Agreements will be discussed in detail in Chapter 13, and a sample BPA is provided as an appendix. Business partner relationships must be addressed front and center in your security program and not glossed as peripheral to it.

When the BPA was signed, many organizations believed that they had effectively washed their hands of responsibility for the employees of the contracted organization. "Let *their* managers ensure that our contractors are abiding by the rules," the healthcare company would say.

In 2013, a key feature of HIPAA went into effect that essentially obligates covered entities to ensure that their contracted employees, or business partners, are complying with all aspects of the HIPAA privacy and security regulations.

In other words, how your business partner handles your patients' PHI *does* matter. How your business partner's computer complies with security standards matters. If your business partner loses a laptop or external hard drive with your patient data, that is *your* data breach and *your* responsibility to report it. Does your health information management coding contractor hire work-from-home employees who use the family computer, full of viruses and malware, to accomplish key business processes for your organization? If so, you are liable for the risk you facilitate.

A Method to the Madness

Healthcare systems everywhere have a common goal—quality outcomes, right? Well, we should assume this, but there is an underlying assumption that the systems are going to make a profit in the process (or go down trying). Even the not-for-profit health systems out there boast large buildings with state-of-the-art technologies. Executives make decent salaries in most cases and, although many providers bemoan the collapse of healthcare as a viable source of income, the reality of the matter is that it is still possible to make a decent living as a doctor or a surgeon. When the federal government stepped in to help healthcare systems implement EMR systems, thereby improving quality outcomes, the same financial drivers remained beneath the surface.

It is simply not viable to continue funding an inefficient system with tax dollars for the long term. By focusing on outcomes, reducing duplicative processes, eliminating readmissions, and mining the data from millions of patients to determine how we might eliminate many of the costly, unnecessary procedures that we pay for day after day, year after year— we just might improve the bottom line.

To do this we need to capture your health data, and we need to capture my health data, and we need to be sure it stays right where it belongs—in the care of the health systems providing our care.

Should our data be used to improve the overall healthcare system? Certainly! Should we expect that our private diagnoses—perhaps cancer one day—will remain confidential and available only to those with whom we chose to share them? Absolutely!

It will, however, take a concerted effort on the part of health systems everywhere to ensure that our health data is handled with no less (and, indeed, I would argue, much *more*) care than our banks use when handling our financial data.

This concerted effort begins by educating healthcare employees about the great responsibility with which they have been entrusted and providing them with the tools they need to do their jobs.

Further Reading

"Notice of Privacy Practices," HHS, http://www.hhs.gov/ocr/privacy/hipaa/understanding/consumers/noticepp.html.

HHS, Office of the Secretary, "Health Insurance Reform: Security Standards; Final Rule," *Federal Register,* 68, no. 34 (2003): 8334–8391, http://www.hhs.gov/ocr/privacy/hipaa/administrative/securityrule/securityrulepdf.pdf.

HHS, "Security Standards: Administrative Safeguards," *HIPAA Security Series,* 2, paper 2 (2005), http://www.hhs.gov/ocr/privacy/hipaa/administrative/securityrule/adminsafeguards.pdf.

"HIMSS Privacy and Security Toolkit," http://www.himss.org/library/healthcare-privacy-security/toolkit?navItemNumber=16480.

Divide and Conquer: Defining Ownership to Develop Solutions

Assembling the Team

Bringing the Right Human Resources to the Table

It's as simple as this. When people don't unload their opinions and feel like they've been listened to, they won't really get on board.

—Patrick Lencioni, *The Five Dysfunctions of a Team: A Leadership Fable*

Getting out of bed that Monday morning was one the most difficult things I had ever done, or at least it seemed that way at the time. I had a dilemma on my hands because the work of the team I was leading was running up against some walls.

We had our timelines and deliverable dates—these weren't going to change— but there was a key stakeholder in the project who was entirely opposed to the direction we were going. I was asked by my director to work with the stakeholder and solicit feedback, but there was a flaw in this plan. Because the stakeholder had no formal role in the project, and therefore no real voice, there was little I could do to enlist her support.

We were at a critical point, and there were two directions the project could go:

1. Our deliverables would fall behind schedule, or worse, grind to a halt.

2. I could find a way to formally involve this key stakeholder and keep things on task.

I took the issue straight to the program director and explained the dilemma that without the support of this individual we would be unable to make any meaningful progress toward our goals.

What happened, in short, was not miraculous, nor was it an ingenious, tactical maneuver. (Manipulation as a human resources management tactic never works, by the way.)

When the stakeholder was invited to the table; provided with a meaningful forum in which to offer concerns, criticisms, and feedback; and given assurances that these were being heard and considered, her adversarial approach suddenly changed. Perhaps she was now indifferent rather than supportive, but roadblocks disappeared and progress resumed.

All of this to say that who is on your team is important, and those who might not share your vision can certainly add a certain depth or character that will enhance and provide value to the team in the long run.

Where to Start

Because you are assembling a team that will tackle issues of privacy and security, specifically as it relates to the EMR system, you would do well to establish some assumptions:

1. First, while you might speak of the collective group of those with an interest in securing the medical record as "the team," you need to understand that there will probably be many teams addressing different areas of privacy and security.

2. Because, as you learned in Chapter 2, there are many different domains in the realm of privacy and security, and each organization is different, no two teams are going to look the same.

3. There are many ways to interpret the law or, more basically, the fiduciary responsibility to protect patient data, so a solution that might be appropriate in one scenario might not be the solution that another organization chooses.

With this in mind, let's look at the key aspects of a team that should, in most cases, be involved in the security of patient data.

From the Top Down

It goes without saying that executive leadership is critical to any privacy and security initiative. Some would identify this "leader" as the privacy officer or chief information security officer (CISO), appointed in accordance with HIPAA.

I would go one step further and almost insist that the top executive in any organization should be aware and fully supportive of privacy and security initiatives. This is not to say that the CEO of a major health system needs to be involved in the minutiae of decisions regarding privacy and security throughout the organization, but unless the CEO is aware of the importance of privacy and security and fully supportive of the operation initiatives to implement privacy and security measures, operational staff will encounter countless unnecessary obstacles and roadblocks.

Keep in mind that health systems are often riddled with iterations of power and influence peddling that would be unheard of in other corners of the corporate world.

Physicians are employees of the system and yet powerful members of the community (and often members of the board). Benefactors to hospitals have their agendas and pet projects and want to ensure that their voices are being heard as well.

When privacy and security initiatives are rammed through ("Because we must!") and these powerbrokers and influence peddlers see them as roadblocks to productivity and barriers to effective patient care, then the CEO is liable to stop these initiatives cold without much discussion.

However, any CEOs worth their salaries will likely support security measures that are thoughtful, meaningful, and well justified (though perhaps not politically popular) if they trust their staff.

If you aren't the person to enlist the support of your chief executive, then perhaps you'll want to do some prodding to see who might be able to ensure that he or she is involved on some level in the privacy and security program. At the very least, you'll want some assurances that the work you are doing is supported from the top down!

The Stakeholders

Although executive support is key, it is likewise important to identify stakeholders throughout your organization. While this might seem like a straightforward task, the positions described next will often vary from organization to organization, so it might take some sleuthing to find out who actually holds the responsibility for some of the key roles in your organization.

Nonetheless, what follows is a general grouping of core disciplines in the healthcare world and how they play a role in the privacy and security space.

Information Technology

IT might seem like a no brainer, but you will want to find the key IT personnel to assist in various aspects of securing the patient record. These include, but are not limited to:

- **Chief security officer:** This is going to be your key resource for understanding current policies and will perhaps be a point person for questions about application configuration or system settings for your EMR system.

- **Security administrators:** These folks will be able to assist you in determining how the organization handles day-to-day security operations and how your EMR system might fit into their workflows.

- **System administrators:** These employees are the ones who will assist you with server settings, workstation settings, system timeouts, password settings, authentication configuration, and more. Get to know your system administrators well!

- **Database administrators:** Where your patient data sits is very important, and you will want to understand how the data is stored, encrypted, backed up, and so forth.

- **Help desk/operations staff:** These are often the people charged with provisioning accounts for operational systems, and they will likely take over once an EMR project is complete. You will want to understand their process to account for them in designing the operational security policies for your EMR.

Health Information Management

The HIM office is charged with ensuring that patient data is handled appropriately, released in accordance with legal requirements, coded according to standards, and stored in compliance with privacy guidelines.

When it comes to privacy, the HIM office will likely be one of your key resources.

- **HIM director:** The director will likely be able to offer an abundance of guidance on what the organization has deemed appropriate or inappropriate in regard to protected health information. Even if your EMR project is relatively new, the HIM office has probably been processing patient charts for years, and they understand the laws as they pertain to patient data.

- **HIM analysts:** When your paper charts are digitized, they can be released to a fax machine, an e-mail address, or another health system instantaneously, and it is important to control the flow of information (*routing*) through accurate contact information such as addresses or fax numbers. Your HIM analysts can help you understand their release of information workflows.

Privacy, Compliance, and Legal

While the three areas of privacy, compliance, and legal are typically not a single office, their functions involve so much overlap that it is helpful to include them under a single heading here.

Chapter 3 discussed briefly how the decisions you make regarding your EMR system and how you build it are often driven by risk tolerance. This is not always a negative thing and must be considered quite frankly.

Would it be easy to provide one view into the system for all users (from housekeeping to physicians) and simply tell employees, "Just click on the buttons that you need to do your job!"? Certainly. But you can be sure that the hospital would be served legal papers in short order when the housekeeper entered the room of a VIP and offered condolences on his recent terminal diagnosis before the physician had had a chance to share the bad news with him.

The following stakeholders who can help you in these sensitive areas are:

- **Corporate counsel:** The health system's attorney team will, perhaps, not want to be involved in the minutiae of your design decisions, but you can be sure that when you have a workflow issue that involves very sensitive information, legal will want to be involved.

- **Compliance officer:** Your compliance officer is often charged with ensuring that your organization abides by rules related to everything from patient restraints to accessibility and cleanliness, and you can be sure that HIPAA and HITECH are terms that the compliance officer knows well.

- **Privacy officer:** The privacy officer is often charged with investigating complaints about misuse of patient charts— such as, "My husband was in the hospital last week, and my neighbor that works at the hospital knows all about his diagnosis! I want to know if she accessed his chart!" You will want to ensure that your privacy officer is involved in building your EMR system and understands how to use audit tools for forensic purposes after you have "gone live."

Clinical

I cannot stress enough how important it is to have the appropriate clinical representation on your privacy and security team. You will need to make sure that you understand what your organization has deemed appropriate access for various levels of clinical staff, and the only way to know this is to have a direct line to the appropriate organizational leaders with this knowledge.

- **Director of nursing/nursing informatics:** This individual will be thoroughly versed in what your non-provider, clinical staff do on a regular basis to accomplish their jobs. Which staff document in the chart? Which staff places orders? What should they be able to see in the chart, and what is not pertinent to their job functions? These are all questions that you must answer if you want to build a system with integrity that incorporate privacy and security throughout.

- **Chief medical information officer:** This officer is typically a physician who knows the physician workflows in your organization and what the physicians need. Furthermore, this individual should know and understand what various providers (think nurse practitioners and anesthesiologists) should be able to do in the system.

Revenue Cycle

Just as clinical representation is vital in how you build access for your nurses and doctors, you will need to ensure that you have representation on the revenue cycle side of the organization as you build access for folks such as schedulers, billers and coders.

You saw that the HIM director will be key in helping you discern how to handle the patient chart; this same person will also be helpful in determining what the coders and HIM staff should be able to do.

You will want to consult with your finance director as you build access for your billing employees, and with managers in your scheduling office as you build access for your schedulers.

What is important to understand here is that since the EMR system is so tightly integrated with scheduling and billing now, it is easy to give users access to areas that are not pertinent to their jobs. Think of a hypothetical clinical user who could see delinquent charges; it is likewise possible to give a billing user full access to a patient chart, and this is something that you will want to avoid (almost always). Be thoughtful about how you deploy elements of the EMR across functional roles.

The Build/Support Team

Depending on where you are in your project—whether fully implemented or beginning an implementation doesn't really matter—you will almost always have a core group of analysts who will be responsible for the *security build* of the application. When I say *security build*, I don't mean to imply lines of code, delicately crafted to make it impervious to hackers.

Remember, most of the application vendors out there have cobbled together applications with their own "code"—remember MUMPS? Our friends at Allscripts, Epic, Cerner, Meditech, and the rest typically give *application analysts* a starting point (think LEGO building blocks, if you will), and these building blocks can be assembled, or *built*, to function in any number of ways.

Security build is, for instance, application access designed for a registered nurse that gives the nurse access to do exactly what a nurse *should* be able to do, *not* what a physician should be able to do—optimized with the buttons and tools that a nurse should have in your organization.

Whether your security analysts are building (new implementation) or supporting your EMR system, you will have people who are charged with ensuring that the application complies with the build and access standards decided on by your organizational stakeholders. These application security analysts will be the backbone of your project or your operational support team and can make or break your team.

Note   A word to the wise: although there are many theories about staffing and support for projects and operations, I cannot stress enough the importance of hiring the right people for these key positions. The indicators that follow, although not foolproof, will certainly improve your chances of staffing your team with the right people. Key words to keep in mind when hiring are *smart*, *driven*, *goal-oriented*, and *analytical*.

The ideal application security analyst should understand the clinical workflows, but doesn't need to have a clinical background. Key strengths of the analyst are:

- **Analytical:** This is an easy one for people to throw out in an interview: "I'm an analytical person." What is more important is the ability to demonstrate how the analyst's analytical skills have solved problems in the past. You will want to see how the analyst has used these skills in conjunction with the advanced functions of standard tools (such as Microsoft Excel) to solve specific problems.

- **Solution implementer:** You will want to be sure that the analyst can take requirements from the abstract, restate them to a customer, and translate them into a deliverable. None of these are easy tasks, and it is doubly challenging to blend the interpersonal and problem-solving elements successfully.

- **Task-oriented:** Your analyst will have many, many tasks and subtasks to complete to build a secure, efficient system for the end-user. If the analyst cannot stay on task, you will run into problems.

- **Successful:** While you don't need someone who has already achieved every one of their goals, you would do well to choose analysts who have an established pattern of setting their sights on goals and achieving them repeatedly.

You can perhaps find a very personable employee in your organization who has done well in several other positions, but an agreeable person who "works well with others" does not necessarily make a good application security analyst (or an application analyst of any sort for that matter—that's free advice for my non–privacy-and-security counterparts out there).

The EMR Security Team

Your EMR will probably need a team of individuals charged with supporting all aspects of EMR security, including, but not limited to, identity and access. A typical team will include some of the following positions:

- **Security lead/security coordinator:** This person is typically charged with coordinating the work of the various application security analysts, account provisioning analysts, and other related support staff. A thoroughly technical worker is required here, but management and people skills are also requisite.

- **Provisioning and support staff:** Although this role might fall to the help desk (or perhaps be entirely auto-mated), some teams will have employees responsible for provisioning accounts and triaging access-related issues. These are normally midlevel technical support staff.

Note The security team for an Epic EMR install will often include a Provider (or SER) lead, who is tasked with maintaining the provider records that are linked to user records. These are not security-related but peripherally affect access and are essentially related to identity. This position is vital to the security team and is truly more of a "data manager" position.

The Security Workgroup

Your EMR support or project team will need a cross-functional group of analysts who represent various parts of the clinical and business applications. To build a cohesive and secure application, you must communicate. The *security workgroup* will be the mechanism for communication among your team members.

How often you meet will be up to you, but you will certainly need to document your work and coordinate your efforts. Your workgroup will certainly be tasked with following organizational project plans and can expect to work with your security stakeholders.

The Security Stakeholders

This group name, *security stakeholders*, is rather generic, but the group itself should not be theoretical. You must have a formally constituted group of stakeholders charged with deciding how the organization will interpret the mandates of HIPAA and the HITECH Act.

HIPAA states that the covered entity must demonstrate how it arrives at its privacy and security practices and how it formalizes accountability for processes and practices. This means a governing body.

What you decide to call this group of people and who is involved are up to your organization. Perhaps it consists of your CISO, director of nursing, director of HIM, compliance officer, and security coordinator. Maybe it's just your CISO and corporate compliance director—though I hope not! The bottom line is that you have to have a group in charge, and you must document the decisions made by this group.

Onward

What is important is that you have assembled a team, you understand your mission (namely, a secure application), and everyone has a voice in the process. Not everyone will be at the table every step of the way, but you need to have your team assembled, and each person needs to understand just how important their role is in ensuring the success of creating a privacy and security program built around the EMR.

When you have the right people at the table, you can begin the tough but worthwhile work ahead of you.

Sifting through the Wreckage

The Security Audit

War is mainly a catalogue of blunders.

—Winston Churchill, The Second World War

Perhaps my parents thought they had a budding architect or engineer on their hands, I'm not sure, but I remember the birthday present quite well. I was probably 10 years old, and as soon as I opened the Erector construction set with all of its seemingly millions of pieces, I couldn't wait to dive in.

After opening another gift or two, a round of "Happy Birthday," and a piece of birthday cake, I was busy surveying everything that the box contained. It wasn't long before I was bolting pieces of metal together, certain that I was going to be able to build the most magnificent contraptions and structures imaginable.

What I soon realized was that the best intentions, even when coupled with some pretty solid creativity, weren't going to lead to a magnificently-Erected anything.

There were lots of pieces and there were some designs that one could follow, but before I was going to be able to dive in and create anything unique, something that I could call my own, I needed to understand how things were done in Erector world. There was an established pattern.

There were designs that led to certain creations. Perhaps there were better ways of doing things, but unless I took the time to understand what I had sitting in front of me, and how things worked (or were supposed to work), I wasn't going to have much success building something new or something better.

When we are presented with something new, we are often inclined to dive in headfirst. A birthday present, a new car, a new piece of technology, or a new project—we are tempted to say, "Let's hit the ground running!"

But as they say, discretion is the better part of valor. To stop, survey what is sitting in front of you, and ensure that you understand all of the pieces before proceeding is certainly the best path forward.

What Are We Waiting For?

We often like to react and "do something" for the sake of securing information assets, but we would do well to take a step back and understand that efforts, if not organized and deliberate, can often be counterproductive.

You can, for instance, require password changes every week, but if your users are permitted to set their passwords to "cat," "dog," or "password," then you are probably just spinning your wheels!

It is important to understand what you have sitting in front of you before you go about the business of planning change and transformation. Without a solid understanding of the core issues and business practices that affect security and privacy, it is pointless to apply patches and bandages, hoping that some effort is better than none.

The Dreaded "A" Word

Before starting down the road of auditing current practices, you have to come to grips with what a security audit is and what it isn't. You've already determined that a good baseline is required before you can make any method out of the madness.

The results of an audit (the work product) will become the toolkit that will act as the foundation of the rest of the work that you have to accomplish in securing the medical record.

With this in mind, it is helpful to understand that as soon as someone begins to investigate current practices in your organization as part of an audit, guards will go up, people will become defensive, and it is possible that the information you need won't be easy to find. A deficient practice is, after all, nothing to be proud of.

What you need to understand before an audit is that it will often uncover deficient practices that came into use under various conditions: those were initially not recognized as deficient; those that were known risks but could not be addressed due to lack of staffing or funding; and those with known flaws that were condoned for the sake of offsetting goals.

Risks are introduced or accepted for any number of reasons, and the purpose of an audit is primarily to document what exists—not the political, practical, or technical reasons behind each risk. When the people you are working with understand that your goal is not to back people into corners, put jobs at risk, or come out on top in a battle to unearth organizational secrets, your job will be much easier.

What's Your Pitch?

Depending on your role in the process of securing the EMR system, you could be the one doing the security audit or risk assessment (as distinguished in subsequent sections), or you might have delegated an appropriate representative from inside or outside of the organization to accomplish the task.

Note The *security risk assessment* is something that helps an organization understand its risks in regard to potential effects. In addition to being an extremely helpful tool in the audit process, it is a requirement in the first stage of meaningful use attestation. Not only must you complete a risk assessment, you must remediate any deficiencies found in a number of key attestation areas. We cover these core areas in more detail later.

Regardless of who is doing the audit, the goal is twofold:

- To complete the audit with as much cooperation from your staff as possible.

- To have a final product that will assist in the process of securing the EMR system.

The message that needs to be conveyed to the employees in the organization who have a stake in securing the privacy and security of patient data needs to be consistent and in keeping with your stated goals.

Whether you are establishing contact via phone or via email, establish your script, and stick to it:

> *Hello, my name is _____, and I am working with the _____ department to understand our current processes as they relate to patient data privacy and security. Every organization has some areas for improvement, and we understand this; we're just hoping to understand what we do now so that we can factor this into our future workflows. I look forward to working with you to get a better understanding of the part that you play in this important task.*

As soon as you contact one person about the needs related to your audit, your colleagues are going to start talking. "So and so called me today and asked me about _____ . Do you know anything about this?"

If your message is clear and consistent, and you ask the same thing of everybody, there will be little suspicion about your intent. People will not think that you are out to sabotage, dig up dirt, or put your nose where it doesn't belong. Establish from the beginning that your goals are the same as your colleagues'—excellent customer service and patient care— and assure them that you are on the same team.

The last thing someone wants is a cold call with requests for information that seem to be getting at something unspecific but foreboding. When this happens, expect guards to go up and the information you receive to be less than helpful.

Who Is Who?

In the previous chapter we spoke about the need to assemble a team to address privacy and security concerns. In the process of auditing your security practices, you will want to be similarly thorough in reaching out across the organization, but the people who will be able to help you answer your questions about security practices will not necessarily be the same ones who will serve on your cross-application/interdisciplinary team to address security concerns.

With this in mind, it is important to know your audience before you reach out with your message and start gathering data.

Note As you begin to establish contacts in your organization, a key aspect of privacy and security is *identity*. Your human resources management office will become an invaluable ally in your attempts to understand the people in your organization, and you would do well to establish good working relationships with key managers in HR as well as your HR information systems (HRIS) administrators.

Breaking it Down

Don't overthink the process just because you are dealing with a digital system. Some of the stakeholders in the privacy and security process are quite separate from the world of IT, and they will be the ones with the answers to your questions in many cases. Let's take a look at some of the functional areas that will help you in the process of your security audit.

- **Physical security/special police:** Although you might overlook the folks who often occupy the basement office or provide a daunting presence in the Emergency Department on busy weekend evenings, it would be a mistake to overlook your security office in the process of your security audit. They can answer questions about the pre-employment security screening, background checks, badge access standards, nonstandard employment termination procedures, physical safeguards around computer equipment and more.

- **Human resources:** The folks in your HR department will be able to assist you with everything from the onboarding process (when a potential employee is considered a "hire"), pre-employment hiring requirements, and processes that might exist between your HR/HRIS division and the IT department.

- **Training:** The training department can help you understand the steps that you take to ensure that employees are trained on technologies, regulations, standards, and corporate policies as they relate to privacy and security. The training program typically has a role in the onboarding of new employees as well as continuing education of existing employees.

- **Risk management and corporate compliance:** The risk management and corporate compliance office is your go-to source for all matters pertaining to how you should be operating and what organizational policies dictate. Their job is to ensure that the organization adheres to the myriad complex regulatory standards and requirements that each healthcare organization is obliged to follow.

- **Internal audit**: Your internal audit office staff is charged with investigating how operational employees are doing their jobs and whether they are performing according to established guidelines or best practices. The internal auditors are frequently able to help you in your attempts to understand current practices in the organization.

- **Legal affairs**: The legal department will be able to provide you with guidance related to what is permitted from a legal standpoint within your organization. Certainly you can do something one way, but that might be entirely inappropriate from a legal standpoint—it is good to have a firm grasp on these issues when grappling with process and practice. Get to know the employees in your legal department, and ask them when you encounter gray areas that require clarification.

- **Health information management**: The HIM office is uniquely positioned in the organization to blend the complex worlds or regulatory compliance and information technology—how the system treats the digital data, transmitting it from one provider to the next, and from one organization to the next, is the domain of the HIM office. Ensuring that data is correct, that demographic information is accurate, and that overall system integrity is maintained is not a small job, and it is not an easy one either.

- **Network operations**: This large, umbrella category within IT covers a host of employees from server administrators and network engineers to help desk employees. What is important here is that the network operations employees will know the processes employed relevant to data storage, access control, user accounts, remote access, and more. What might make your job more difficult is the process of trying to find out how all of these pieces fit together (or if they fit together). Often one person is charged with a task and has no knowledge of what others in the organization do when it comes to other pieces of the puzzle.

- **Information security**: Hopefully your organization will have an information security officer (or other similarly charged employee) who is responsible for all aspects of information security in your organization. The HIPAA Security rule requires such a position in each healthcare organization, and although this designee might be an office manager with yet another hat, it is important to know where the buck stops when it comes to information security at your site. This individual will, or should, be able to address matters of policy related to information security, privacy, and compliance, and to tell you what initiatives or projects are underway to address areas that are not yet mature.

- **Everyone else**: This might seem like a vague category, but it is important to understand that you need to be open to finding answers to your questions in unexpected places. Perhaps you have answered all of your process questions. You know that HR enters all of new employees into the HRIS system on the first of the month, the help desk analysts create all appropriate user accounts, and the system engineers apply all appropriate network permissions, but the question remains, "How does the end-user get credentials on the first day on the job?" In speaking to the administrative assistant one day, perhaps you find the missing link: "Oh, I get those from the help desk in an e-mail, and I write them on a sticky note, and put them on the user's monitor the night before they start." Don't leave any stone unturned, and don't assume that obvious flaws in a process will be apparent to everyone!

Note   Notice the pattern here—no aspect of the privacy and security process can be considered in isolation. What one person does affects the rest, and this has ripple effects all the way down to EMR security. In the process of coordinating EMR privacy and security, it is imperative to build relationships and, above all, understand process.

Brass Tacks

With all of this information at hand, it is important to understand that the audit process will allow you to systematically evaluate data you gather, processes you observe, conversations you have, and documents/policies you review.

However, it is not enough to gather data. A lot of data, whether in a file folder or on a network file share, is still just a lot of data. An audit is not an audit until that data is collected, evaluated based on a set of expert opinions, and compiled into a report.

The purpose of the audit report is to evaluate the effectiveness of current controls and processes and further recommend a set of corrective measures to bring your organization into alignment with best practices, mitigating risk in the process.

Tools of the Trade

You might ask the question, "Where do I start?" I'm sure there are countless others right beside you wondering the same thing.

Fortunately, the road to the healthcare security audit has been well traveled over the years, and there are some tools that can be used, preventing most of us from having to reinvent the wheel, so to speak.

Let's take a look at the specific language provided by HHS:

> The Security Management Process standard in the Security Rule requires organizations to "[i]mplement policies and procedures to prevent, detect, contain, and correct security violations." (45 C.F.R. § 164.308(a)(1).) Risk analysis is one of four required implementation specifications that provide instructions to implement the Security Management Process standard. Section 164.308(a)(1)(ii)(A) states: RISK ANALYSIS (Required). Conduct an accurate and thorough assessment of the potential risks and vulnerabilities to the confidential, integrity, and availability of electronic protected health information held by the [organization].[1]

Not only does the HIPAA Security Rule require a thoughtful risk analysis for all organizations storing protected health information, but demonstrated evidence that the organization has completed such a risk assessment is required to receive federal funds under the Stage 1 Meaningful Use Incentives provided by the Affordable Care Act.

So much for a regulation without teeth! The link of substantial monetary funds is now directly tied to evidence that you have thoroughly evaluated your organization's processes and procedures for risks related to privacy and security. Otherwise you don't get the federal funds tied to meaningful use for EMR systems that you have implemented.

---

[1]US Department of Health & Human Services, "Guidance on Risk Analysis Requirements under the HIPAA Security Rule." Posted July 14, 2010. http://www.hhs.gov/ocr/privacy/hipaa/administrative/securityrule/rafinalguidancepdf.pdf

We Get By with a Little Help from Our Friends ...

HHS is deliberately vague about what an organization is required to do to meet the requirements of a security risk assessment. They will not tell you what this has to look like, who has to perform the risk assessment, or what your final report should like.

Note   Keep in mind that the risk assessment is a tool to help with the audit (the audit produces findings and recommendations). Although an audit should be independent, don't let the fact that you might be performing the audit for your organization diminish the independent nature of your work—the fact that you are working to determine the propriety of security practices in functional areas across the organization (all of these cannot fall under a single business owner) elevates the objectivity of the task at hand. If you are able to work with an independent auditor to accomplish this important task, you will be ahead of the game, learning (perhaps) more than you would from the inside.

According to HHS, you simply must complete a risk assessment, and it must thoroughly meet the requirements outlined. Unhelpful, right? Perhaps it seems so, until you do a little more digging and realize that HHS has facilitated an industry working group called the *National Learning Consortium* (NLC), which further supports a specific task force devoted to the domain of privacy and security.

This group produced a resource that is invaluable in the healthcare IT security space and an essential tool for anyone charged with privacy and security oversight. The *HIT Security Risk Assessment Tool* is a Microsoft Excel Workbook (macro-enabled) that guides the auditor through the process of evaluating privacy and security practices in the healthcare enterprise.

Note   The easiest way to find the risk assessment tool is to perform a browser search for the complete phrase "HIT Security Risk Assessment Tool" (for the purposes of discussion from this point forward, we simply refer to it as the *Risk Toolkit*). When you find the link, be sure that you are downloading the Excel file from the healthit.gov website, and enable the macro content on launching the file.

There are many ways to accomplish an audit, and this book isn't about to provide a comprehensive evaluation of audit methodologies (you can read books on this topic if you are interested).

What I propose here is that the Risk Toolkit provided by HHS can be used to facilitate the audit process and get you where you need to be as you work to secure your EMR system. The step-by-step process outlined in the toolkit can help you understand the path you are traveling, and, as you begin to enter values in the workbook, you will start to see how all of the pieces fit together.

Once you ask questions, find the answers, and plug in the values, you will see where some of your risks are, where your gaps are, and what recommendations will need to be in your audit report.

Diving In

Once you have downloaded the Risk Toolkit, you'll want to familiarize yourself with the two tabs titled "How to Complete the Forms" and "Risk Guidance" (see Figure 5-1).

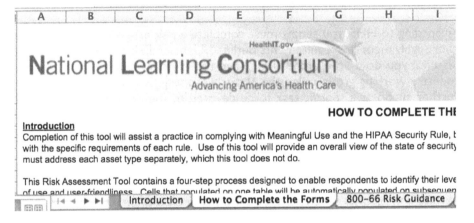

Figure 5-1. The Risk Toolkit

If you were thinking that a spreadsheet would simply provide an assortment of fields to populate with values, numbers, and data, then think again. There is a wealth of information that will help the novice auditor and the veteran alike through the process of performing a security risk assessment in the healthcare space.

You will note on the first tab that the Risk Toolkit is based on standards set forth by the National Institutes of Standards and Technology (NIST), and you would do well to familiarize yourself with these NIST standards. When you see the HIPAA rule, or other HHS document, reference a seemingly cryptic alpha-numeric value such as 164.308(a)(1)(ii)(A), this is not an attempt to obfuscate what could have been stated simply, but a point of reference to information security standards set forth by NIST.

HHS has tried *not* to reinvent the wheel when it comes to implementing privacy and security standards, referring instead to what the information security industry has already accepted as normative.

When you see these references, venture out to the NIST website and do a little more reading. The better equipped you are with the data about why standards are being implemented (that often lead to changes people resent or resist), the better equipped you will be in your attempts to enlist allies in support of your security program.

Four Steps

The Risk Toolkit outlines a logical flow for completing the risk analysis, beginning with some preparatory steps and moving through a three-step process that leads eventually to a concise risk register that can be used as the basis for an audit report.

The Preparation Phase and Inventory

The Preparation Tab of the Risk Toolkit is listed as optional, but I would suggest that you do not overlook this important step in the audit process. What you will gain here is invaluable to the risk assessment process, and you will find that this Inventory of Assets will be a point of reference you will use repeatedly in the future.

The questionnaire is straightforward and requires you to take an inventory of all information assets in the organization with a particular mind to the question, "Does this device or software package enable or facilitate the storage or transmission of ePHI?"

In other words, is digital protected health information stored or transmitted by means of this asset? If the answer is yes, then the organization must give an account for how it is managing that information asset.

Let's take a look at some possible entries in the Inventory of Assets tab of the Risk Toolkit. In the example that appears in Figure 5-2, we've begun the process of entering various information assets that the organization should consider in the development of its security program.

A	B	C
Asset Type	**Does this asset process, store or transmit EPHI?**	**People/Process or Technology Asset?**
Fax Machine	Yes	People and Processes
Multi-Function Copier/Scanner/Fax	Yes	People and Processes
Smart Phones (iPhone/Android)	Yes	People and Processes
Microsoft Excel	Yes	Technology
iPad/Tablets	Yes	People and Processes
iPax Smart Imaging Software	Yes	Technology

How to Complete the Forms   Inventory (Preparation)   800–66 Risk

Figure 5-2. Inventory of Assets

Notice that the list includes everything from company-issued (or perhaps personally owned) smart phones to spreadsheet software. The devices, the things that people use, are placed in the "People/Process" category, and the software that simply has the capability to store data is placed in the "Technology" category.

This inventory process should be carried out until every asset or type of asset is listed and categorized so that they can be included in your security program. Note that our primary concern is with the security of the EMR system; while an EMR might have been an island at one point, smart phones, tablets, and fax machines are all integrated into the fabric of these systems. There is no longer a clear line between a device and the EMR, and without a comprehensive picture of what kind of assets an organization is dealing with, we can't get a handle on where patient data begins and ends.

Step 1: The Screening Questions

The first section after the asset inventory is titled "Screening Questions," and it walks you through a set of core questions related to privacy and security practices in your organization.

As you think back to all of the departments and organizational contacts that we listed at the beginning of this chapter, you will see how these various functional areas come into play at this point in the risk assessment. You will be asked to answer questions about the person charged with the duties of security officer, the processes employed for terminations, the process used for pre-employment screenings, controls for secure areas, and more.

You will be asked to evaluate each of these domains with a response of "Addressed," "Not Addressed," or "Partially Addressed."

To the right of your response, you will be offered an opportunity to comment on the response with information that will be helpful in your final report. For instance, in Figure 5-3, when asked in question 1.1, "Has your organization formally appointed a central point of contact for security coordination?" since we answered yes, it is helpful to list the name of the chief information security officer and the date he was appointed.

	Topic	Question	Response	Threat Vulnerability Statement	People/ Processes	Technology
1. Security Program						
1.1	*Roles & Responsibilities*	[1.1] Has your organization formally appointed a central point of contact for security coordination? a) If so, whom, and what is their position within the organization? b) Responsibilities clearly documented? i.e. job descriptions, information security policy	**Addressed**	Management has not defined responsibilities for the information security program. [TVS001]	James Smith assigned as Chief Information Security Officer (CISO) on 12/15/2011.	N/A
1.2	*External Parties*	[1.2] Do you work with third parties, such as IT service providers, that have access to your patient's information? a) Does your organization have Business Associate agreements in place with these third parties? i.e. REC, IT Vendor, EHR Vendor, etc. b) If not, what controls does your organization have in place to monitor and assess third parties? i.e. Logging of VPN connections, EHR logs, etc	**Not Addressed**	Security breaches occur when dealing with third parties due to a lack of security considerations in the related third party agreement. [TVS002]	Business Partner Agreements not signed/filed - need to address as soon as possible.	
2. Security Policy						

How to Complete the Forms / Inventory (Preparation) / 800-66 Risk Guidance / Practice Summary / Screening Questions (Step 1) / People and Processes (Step 2a) / Technology (Step 2b)

Figure 5-3. Question 1.1 response examples

To complete this section properly and thoroughly, you will need to read through each section and question and determine who (from your list of security contacts) can help you determine the answer. Once you have organized these questions, and assigned a subject matter expert to help you address the issue, you are ready to begin the process of gathering data.

Walk though the series of questions, responding to each query with an appropriate response and comment(s) to each of the following security domains:

1. Security Program

2. Security Policy

3. Risk Management and Compliance

4. Training and Awareness

5. Personnel Security

6. Physical Security

7. Network Security

8. Logical Access

9. Operations Management

10. Incident Management

11. Business Continuity Management

Once you complete the answers to each query in this section, you can move on to Step 2.

Step 2a: People and Processes

The second section that you will need to complete is broken down into two sections, the first of which is titled "People and Processes." Here you will be asked to evaluate the human-related processes for what the Risk Toolkit calls "Effectiveness of Control." In essence, you are making a judgment call regarding the effectiveness of your controls, or lack of controls, related to a given security process or discipline.

In the example in Figure 5-4, you will notice that the column titled "Existing Control" pulls data that you previously entered in step 1. When you begin to populate the values for "Existing Control Effectiveness" in this phase, the logic built into the workbook will start to evaluate your risk ratings in regard to the domains and disciplines (or processes) being evaluated.

Asset Management Category	Threat-Vulnerability Statement	Recommended Control Measures	Existing Control	Existing Control Effectiveness	Exposure Potential	Likelihood	Impact	Risk Rating
Security Program	Management has not defined responsibilities for the information security program. [TVS001]	All information security responsibilities are clearly documented . This is to ensure timely, safe and effective handling of all situations, administration user accounts- including additions, deletions, and modifications. [RCM001] - Ensure responsibilities are formalized within	James Smith assigned as Chief Information Security Officer (CISO) on 12/15/2011.	Effective			High	
Risk Management & Compliance	Information around risks and related control options are not presented to management before management decisions are made. [TVS004]	Risk assessments are conducted to identify, quantify, prioritize and manage risks. The prioritization is accomplished by creating and using criteria for risk acceptance and objectives which are important to the organization. [RCM004] - Ensure this risk assessment is accurate with	- REC helping to start the risk assessment process by using this spreadsheet as a foundation for the risk assessment as well as risk management plan. - No prior risk assessments	Not Effective	High	Likely	High	Medium
Risk Management & Compliance	Legislative, statutory, regulatory or contractual obligations related to security are violated due to lack of controls. [TVS005]	Controls, which are applicable to each situation, have been applied to avoid violations of any legal obligations (e.g. statutory, regulatory, or contractual), and of any security requirements. Access controls could be door locks or computer passwords, while other controls could be	- Working with the REC helps to identify new laws and regulations due to the training and guidance with the REC team - State breach guidance also	Effective		Not Likely	High	Low
Network Security	Technical vulnerabilities are exploited to gain inappropriate or unauthorized access to information systems due to lack of controls for those vulnerabilities.	Timely information about technical vulnerabilities of information systems being used is obtained, the organization's exposure to the vulnerabilities is evaluated and appropriate measures are taken to address the associated risk. [RCM013] - Vulnerability testing should be performed regularly to obtain information bout technical	- No vulnerability testing has been completed.	Not Effective	High	Very Likely	High	High

How to Complete the Forms / Inventory (Preparation) / 800-66 Risk Guidance / Practice Summary / People and Processes (Step 2a) / Screening Que

Figure 5-4. People and Processes

You will see the far right column of your workbook begin to light up with greens, reds, and yellows depending on how you answer these questions. At this point in the process you are starting to see how your information gathering leads to a meaningful analysis, which can then be conveyed into findings in your audit report when all is said and done.

Once you have completed everything under the People and Processes section, you can move on to the Technology Section.

Step 2b: Technology

The next section covers technologies instead of human-related processes and assigns a logically based risk rating to teach technology (or domain) based on the answers that you previously supplied.

The snapshot in Figure 5-5 shows only part of the data rendered in this section, but it gives you an idea of what you will be seeing as the Risk Toolkit provides you with insights into security risks in your organization.

A	E	F	G	I	L
Asset Management Category	Existing Control Effectiveness	Exposure Potential	Likelihood	Impact	Risk Rating
Risk Management & Compliance	Not Effective	High	Likely	High	Medium
Personnel Security	Effective	Medium	Not Likely	High	Low
Physical Security	Partially Effective	High	Very Likely	High	High

Figure 5-5. Technology risk ratings

Step 3: Findings and Remediations

The final section collates the data that you provide along with the risk ratings generated by the workbook to offer a comprehensive listing of findings. The top of your Findings and Remediations tab will provide you will a snapshot of risks that you will need to address (see Figure 5-6).

Number of High Risks	6
Number of Medium Risks	5
Total Number of High and Medium Risks	11

Figure 5-6. Risks to address (summary)

Notice that the risks that were rated "Low" are not included here in the summary findings tab. You will not want to gloss entirely the low-risk findings (some of these are areas that an organization will certainly need to improve on). The reality is that low-risk security concerns often fall into categories that should be addressed but are unlikely to happen, and are therefore given little to no weight when it comes to a security program.

Everyone understands that resources are limited, and in the case of a security risk assessment, this is no exception. There just isn't time to address every potential concern.

The goal is to look at those domains where the risk and impact are substantial (causing harm to the organization or the customers you serve) and remediate and address those as quickly as possible.

Below the summary of medium and high risks, you will find detail related to each of these risks (see Figure 5-7). Your notes, as well as information that will help you in the remediation process, are included here. This section can be used as a task list of action items from which to work after the audit is complete.

Risks Found (High and Medium Only)	Risk Rating	Existing Control Measures Applied
People and Processes		
Information around risks and related control options are not presented to management before management decisions are made. [TVS004]	Medium	- REC helping to start the risk assessment process by using this spreadsheet as a foundation for the risk assessment as well as risk management plan. - No prior risk assessments conducted
Technical vulnerabilities are exploited to gain inappropriate or unauthorized access to information systems due to lack of controls for those vulnerabilities. [TVS013]	High	- No vulnerability testing has been completed.

Figure 5-7. Details on risks

Finally, take note that there are fields where you can highlight the steps that you plan to take to remediate the risks discovered, as well as identify the primary owner who will be addressing these risks (Figure 5-8). The target date for remediation is added so that you can associate goals and follow-up with the business owner who has been tasked with addressing the risk.

Owner	Remediation Steps	Target Date
James Smith - CISO	Develop a Risk Management plan, and present to leadership for approval. Then communicate this to business owners and operational staff.	4/9/15
Mary Williams - Security Architect	Develop a comprehensive patch management program, and monitor for effectivness.	11/13/14

Figure 5-8. Remediation steps, owners, and target dates

Putting It All Together

Once you have completed the risk assessment, you will have something in your hands to help you address EMR security, but you still have to put the pieces together.

Perhaps you gleaned insights during your conversations that weren't thoughtfully displayed in the Risk Toolkit. You'll want to cull those out and put those in narrative form in your *audit report*. Remember that your opinion and findings are the work product of your research and the data that you gathered. You can't require your organization to take action on each of your recommendations, nor can you make everyone agree with each of your opinions, but when you take the time to do the work an audit entails, you owe it to your employer and the patients you serve to put the pieces together in the end.

The Risk Toolkit and all of the detail from it should be included in your final audit report, and you can include any number of supplemental materials that you think might be helpful to those who will use the report. External auditors, security personnel, future employees, and others will appreciate the detail you include, as it will become a benchmark against which to gauge progress.

A Final Note on the Meaningful Use Risk Assessment

As discussed in this chapter, to "attest" to meaningful use of your EMR system, you must demonstrate that you have completed a risk assessment, and the Risk Toolkit meets this requirement.

However, meaningful use requirements are quite specific in regard to controls (and tests for these controls) within your network and in your EMR system. With this in mind, to comply with this aspect of the Meaningful Use Requirement (Stage I), you will need to follow the procedures that follow and include these EMR-specific test results with your risk assessment findings.

The following eight "Meaningful Use Quality Measures" are security specific, and are listed here with their corresponding logical measure name. Included with each of these measures is a corresponding NIST test document that can be followed to demonstrate compliance:

1. **MU 170.302.q, Access Control**: This quality measure is related to the control of unique users to appropriate activities in the EMR system. (Test procedure: http://healthcare.nist.gov/docs/ 170.302.o_AccessControl_v1.0.pdf)

2. **MU 170.302.p, Emergency Access**: This quality measure is related to the availability of patient data from the EMR during unplanned downtime. (Test procedure: http://healthcare.nist.gov/docs/ 170.302.p_EmergencyAccess_v1.0.pdf)

3. **MU 170.302.q, Automatic Logoff**: This quality measure is related to EMR system's ability to automatically terminate inactive sessions to prevent unauthorized access to patient data.(Test procedure:http://healthcare.nist. gov/docs/170.302.q_AutomaticLogOff_v1.0.pdf)

4. **MU 170.302.r, Audit Log**: This quality measure is related to the EMR system's ability to record transaction data related to time, date, patient ID, and user ID. (Test procedure: http://healthcare.nist.gov/docs/ 170.302.r_AuditLog_v1.0.pdf)

5. **MU 170.302.s, Integrity**: This quality measure relates to the integrity of data when exchanged between your EMR system and another party's EMR, ensuring that the data is not altered as it traverses from one system to the other. (Test procedure: http://healthcare.nist.gov/docs/ 170.302.s_Integrity_v1.0.pdf)

6. **MU 170.302.t, Authentication**: This quality measure is concerned with the manner in which accounts are permitted to access or blocked from accessing the EMR system based on account settings. (Test procedure: http://healthcare.nist.gov/docs/ 170.302.t_Authentication_v1.0.pdf)

7. **MU 170.302.u, General Encryption**: This quality measure is concerned with the encryption of data in the various components that store ePHI within the EMR system. (Test procedure: http://healthcare.nist.gov/ docs/170.302.u_GeneralEncryption_v1.0.pdf)

8. **MU 170.302.v, Encryption HIE:** This quality measure is concerned with the end-to-end encryption of data in a health information exchange (HIE). (Test procedure: http://healthcare.nist.gov/docs/ 170.302.v_EncryptionHIE_v1.0.pdf)

You will need to test your EMR system for these quality measures and include your test process and findings with your risk assessment. In certain domains such as encryption HIE and integrity, it might be sufficient to supply thorough documentation (line and verse) from your vendor in lieu of testing these technologies on your own.

Armed and Ready?

To this point, you have been covering a lot of background, gathering data, and getting your ducks in a row. Again, I cannot stress enough the importance of having a plan before diving in to do the actual work.

With this in mind, you are almost ready to start working with some solutions. But there is a little more legwork to do. The next and final chapter in Part 2 will cover the last steps that you need to take before diving into the steps of actually securing the EMR.

Further Reading

HealthIT.gov, "How to Implement EHRs: Step 2: Plan Your Approach," HealthIT.gov, http://www.healthit.gov/providers-professionals/ehr-implementation-steps/step-2-plan-your-approach.

HHS, "Guidance on Risk Analysis Requirements under the HIPAA Security Rule," HHS.gov, July 14, 2010, http://www.hhs.gov/ocr/privacy/hipaa/administrative/securityrule/rafinalguidancepdf.pdf.

HealthIT.gov, "About the Health IT National Learning Consortium," HealthIT.gov, http://www.healthit.gov/providers-professionals/national-learning-consortium

Office of the National Coordinator for HIT, "Guide to Privacy and Security of Health Information, Chapter 4: Integrating Privacy and Security," HealthIT.gov, http://www.healthit.gov/sites/default/files/pdf/privacy/privacy-and-security-guide-chapter-4.pdf.

Review Your Policies and Develop a Plan

Strategies for Success

Plans are worthless, but planning is everything.

—Dwight D. Eisenhower

You have identified your partners in your project, you know who the business owners are, and you understand some of your risks. Before you begin to implement the changes that will lead to a secure EMR system, you will want to ensure you have a roadmap that will assure success.

You will need to know not only how you are going to get from point A to point B. but also what kind of resources you have to move you along that path, what your organization's risk tolerance is, what legwork has already been done, and what you are expected to deliver. Without clear answers to these questions, you will be spinning your wheels and making incremental progress at best.

Out of the Archives

Whether it seems like it or not, most organizations are not starting from scratch when it comes to privacy and security policies. You might ask someone about a process or policy only to receive a vague noncommittal reply. Obviously, you think, there is *no* established policy for this process in our organization!

What is more often the case than not is that an office manager, security officer, CIO, or human resources officer has already established a policy related to the process you are concerned about. There is likely a file cabinet, network file share, or intranet server somewhere in your organization with a document (perhaps out of date) offering some guidance about how the organization intended to handle the matter at hand.

Your task is often to round these documents up and determine when they were last updated and who owns them in their present state. This might be no easy task. Nonetheless, it is important to survey what has been implemented and already decided before you begin your work, so that you don't waste time, or worse, duplicate the efforts of someone else in the organization who might be working on a similar project.

No Man Is an Island

Whatever title you have been given—security project manager, security manager, security coordinator, privacy officer—doesn't matter. Your job is to ensure that privacy and security are a common thread woven into the fabric of how your organization does business.

The best way to do this from the outset is to operate within the context of your *project management office* (PMO). By taking your efforts to the PMO early in the process, you will be given access their methodologies and resources and, with any luck, your security project(s) will be given visibility within the PMO and integrated into their *enterprise project plan*.

The benefit here is that your initiatives to secure the EMR system end-to-end will receive a project sponsor—most likely the CISO, but perhaps the CIO—and efforts that might have been be stalled by bureaucracy will be hastened along by the mandate of organizational leadership. The benefit of an organized approach to security initiatives cannot be overestimated.

Note Regardless of the strength of your organization's PMO, executive support for security initiatives is essential to securing the EMR. You will encounter countless roadblocks without executive support, which is essential to any security program.

I can think back to countless security initiatives that should have been rubber-stamped—they were so basic. But trying to push the changes through was met with opposition time after time, and I couldn't determine the source of the resistance.

"I'm just trying to require some very basic security standards. This is nothing revolutionary, and is exactly what 99 percent of the IT world has been doing for the last 10 to 15 years!" I would say.

But after countless meetings and too many emails, what I discovered was that since leadership was not advocating for the changes that needed to happen, the end-users were resistant. The changes, though small in the grand scheme of things, were an inconvenience, and there was no clear message from the top saying, "I understand your reservations, but this is the right thing to do for our patients and to safeguard our data."

When the message from the top changed and came into line with the technical change that was being advanced, there was a dramatic change in the user population. Not everybody was on board with the perceived inconvenience that was being imposed, but the resistance to change waned, and eventually the changes were accepted for the best and life went on.

When security initiatives begin and end in the PMO and the PMO is strongly supported by leadership and executives, petty issues that tend to impede progress (and you can be sure that privacy and security issues will cause a host of these issues to rise to the surface) can generally be avoided.

Laying Out the Plan

Whether you are working with your PMO or developing your project plan yourself, you will need to be realistic about what you are trying to accomplish. Find the resources that will help you accomplish your tasks and set deadlines for meeting your goals.

Using a *Gantt chart* tool such as Microsoft Project is helpful, but you can plan your project with a spreadsheet or simple document as long as you don't lose sight of your tasks and deadlines.

Key in this phase is identifying all of your action items from your risk register. Determine what is in scope for your security project, and lay out a plan of attack for addressing these concerns.

Next, you will want to look ahead in this book to lay out a plan for some of the key items related to EMR system security. Though we haven't covered these areas in detail, we offer guidance in the following six areas grouped as *security solutions*:

- Identity and access management
- Application design
- Physical and environmental safeguards
- Systemwide and client-based security configuration
- Securing patient data
- The human element: education and audit

When you have taken the time to plan your approach to the security project, you'll be in a great position to begin the work of securing the EMR and ensuring the integrity of the patient data that has been entrusted to your care.

Beginning the Work

With the foundation laid, you should be ready to tackle the real work of implementing security solutions. The key as you press forward is to stop along the way and take in your surroundings when things get murky. There truly is a mountain of new information out there for most people to digest, and the only way to do well at the task is to be sure you understand what you are working on before moving on to the next step.

Regulations change on an annual basis, and the technologies that healthcare systems adopt evolve almost as rapidly. Search the Internet; the HHS website is a treasure trove of information. Use your vendor's knowledge base, and enlist the support of those who have been there longer than you.

I cannot stress enough the importance of doing the job well. Always keep in mind the extremely sensitive nature of the "bits and bytes" you are handling—those test results that you just downloaded to your laptop are a young mother's new cancer diagnosis. That blood draw on your computer screen contains information that will be devastating for someone in less than 24 hours. Your job is to keep that information safe and to treat it with the utmost care.

Now it's time to get busy with the work of securing that data.

Sustainable Solutions

Identity and Access Management

Know Your User Base

> So it is said that if you know your enemies and know yourself, you can win a hundred battles without a single loss. If you only know yourself, but not your opponent, you may win or may lose. If you know neither yourself nor your enemy, you will always endanger yourself.
>
> —Sun Tzu, *The Art of War*

A call comes in, and the tone is urgent. "A VIP was admitted to the hospital for several hours last week, and this morning the news outlets across the country are all carrying stories related to his medical condition," says the compliance officer on the other end of the phone. The patient's lawyer contacted the hospital to complain that someone shared information about the patient's diagnosis, and they are threatening legal action.

A quick review of the patient's chart history shows that the attending physician and the nurse assigned to the patient's room both accessed the chart at times that seem appropriate to the stay; the compliance officer said that these should be the only users in the chart. There is a third user listed as having accessed the patient's chart on four occasions in the 12 hours after the patient was discharged. You call the charge nurse for that floor and ask if she recognizes the name. She doesn't.

You go into to the human resources system and search for the user's name, and you still don't find a match. After searching through all of the credentialing systems with no luck, you turn to Internet search engines and find seven people with that name in your city, but you have no way of making a positive identification. Without a clue about the identity of this mystery third user, you are forced to call corporate compliance and tell them the news. Yes, a third individual accessed the VIP's chart, but you have no way to identify this person. The patient's attorney has already requested a copy of the *legal medical record* (LMR), including a list of all users who accessed the chart. The hospital has no way of telling who this user was, or if there was a valid reason for this user to access the chart.

■ **Note**   Typically in an organization, the EMR system is just one of a myriad of systems where identity information is housed. You need to understand the limits of your organization's identity systems and work to find a solution for identity management that is sustainable and, most importantly, allows an auditable record of user activity in the patient chart.

Scenarios like this one happen all too often, and they highlight the importance of having a strong identity system that allows the organization to know who has access to its systems and what they should have access to. Weak identity systems can open an organization up to lawsuits and fines that are far more costly than the expense of putting effective controls in place. Unfortunately, many organizations don't invest the time and resources required to fix the problem of identity and access until it is too late. In the end, the financial cost of a lawsuit pales in comparison to the expense of losing public trust and business in the wake of negative press.

Know Yourself

A good principle in the world of identity management is "know yourself." In other words, get a handle on who is in your organization. Once you positively identify who *should* have access to your systems, it is much easier to begin the process of identifying who *should not* have access to your systems.

A good and quick way to test the current state of your identity system is to perform a cursory search for a common last name, say, Jones or Smith. If your organization is like many others, there will be several users with identical names—perhaps "Mary Jones" or "John Smith." (My apologies to those in small organizations with a limited user base—be thankful that this limitation makes the task of identity management that much easier for you.) Using the tools available to you, can you clearly identify these two individuals with the same name? Do you know if these two accounts are actually for different people? Is this the same person with duplicate accounts? If you needed to contact either of these users about an issue with their account, would you have enough information to do so?

If you answered yes to these questions, congratulations! You are probably doing much of the work of identity management already. If you answered no or "I don't know," you are not alone. But you have demonstrated the obvious need to do a better job at knowing yourself.

The solution to identity management woes is not, as many people might think, to add identity information such as address and phone number to the user records in your EHR system. Perhaps there is a place for address, phone number, and email address in the user record of your EHR. A well-meaning person might attempt to populate all of those identifying fields. But is this the best place to start?

The most important piece of information that you can place in any user record is a *unique identifier* that points to a *source of truth.* In other words, you don't need to keep all sorts of demographic information in a system as long as there is a pointer to a system where the accurate, up-to-date information resides. After all, once you populate address information in the user records, the data loses its currency as soon as a single person moves or gets a new phone number.

This brings us to an important principle: *Always identify the systems that will serve as your sources of truth for identity purposes, and reference those systems when verifying identity information.* Perhaps the source of truth is your *human resources information system* (HRIS), or maybe it is a combination of your HRIS and medical credentialing system. The important thing to remember is that these systems will be updated by their administrators, who are charged with keeping accurate identity information, and other systems should point to these, either programmatically or logically. Let's take a look at several scenarios.

Identity Mapping Basics

In the first scenario (Figure 7-1), the user record database (or table) in the EHR system contains a user ID called JSMITH. Notice that the only data in the user record beyond the user name is a field called "Employee ID." With only these two bits of information and access to the enterprise HRIS employee database, we can make the correlation between JSMITH in the medical record system and John Smith in the HRIS system. The foundations of identity management can be as simple as maintaining a unique identifier that points to your source of truth—in this case, the HRIS system.

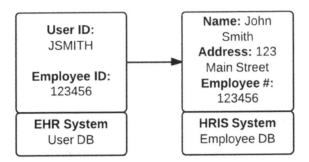

Figure 7-1. Identity mapping scenario in which the EHR system maps to the HRIS system

In the second scenario (Figure 7-2), your EHR system's user database is linked to an enterprise directory service, such as Microsoft's Active Directory or Novell's eDirectory—both of which are implementations of the standards-based *Lightweight Directory Access Protocol* (LDAP). In this scenario, the EHR system is configured to reference an LDAP server for user authentication. The EHR system looks at the user ID and finds a match on the LDAP server before authenticating the user and allowing access to the medical record. Notice that the LDAP server is still not our source of truth, but it contains the information required to make the final connection to our HRIS system, the source of truth.

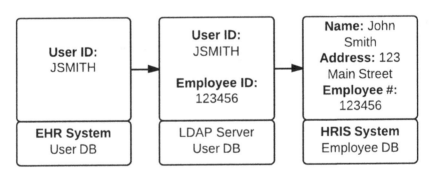

Figure 7-2. Identity mapping scenario in which the EHR system maps to the LDAP server

The first step in ensuring that you know who has access to your data is to make sure that you have a firm link to your source of truth. Once this most basic piece of information is in the user record, the foundation of the identity management system has been laid.

Process, Process, Process

The examples in the preceding section identify an essential element in your account provisioning process: namely, populating unique identifiers. Remember, your unique identifier should not be limited to your HRIS employee ID; you aren't going to have an employee ID for everyone who needs access to your systems. Perhaps the source of truth for physicians and other providers is your credentialing system. Vendors and contractors will not be in your HRIS system or your credentialing system; you will need another unique identifier for them.

The process you put in place should dictate that a unique identifier is required for all account provisioning, but the unique identifier you use is entirely up to you. The end result should be a link to your source of truth, whatever that might be. In the case of vendors and contractors, perhaps this will be a spreadsheet maintained by the employee who manages your *business partner agreements (see Chapter 14)*. The process you implement should clearly identify your identity-mapping scheme so that, when necessary, you can tell exactly who has access to your data.

But account provisioning is only part of your process. What happens to a user record when employees leave the organization, and how do you ensure that access is terminated appropriately on departure? Your *deprovisioning process* should account for termination workflows as well.

Note   Know your processes and document them thoroughly. You should become familiar with "swimlaning" your provisioning and deprovisioning processes so that the responsibilities of each business owner are clearly defined. Use flowchart software such as Visio, Smartdraw, or online programs such as Lucidchart to get your processes documented and organized.

Imagine that your process involves reception of daily emails from the HRIS system with a list of all terminations. In addition, your medical staff office sends a monthly update of privilege revocations, and your business office notifies you as needed when a vendor's contract is revoked. Your deprovisioning process should provide your connection, in reverse, from the source of truth to the systems in your care. You must document your processes thoroughly, and account for all variables in your organization. The only way to document your processes thoroughly is to know them, and to know them you often have to do a lot of digging.

The provisioning and deprovisioning processes will catch most of your users, but there will always be a negligent manager who forgets to send a termination notice for a vendor, or a contractor who left the organization but somehow fell through the cracks and remains in the system. How do you account for and manage these?

Periodic Access and Inactivity Review

Since you will implement a process for provisioning and deprovisioning user accounts from your sources of truth, you will need a way to review the access of other users in your system who might not fall into tidy buckets. These users' accounts can be validated or disabled by using a process of *periodic access review*.

Periodic access review is a practice that should be employed at least annually for all users in your systems. The review should begin by pulling a point-in-time extract of all users along with the access assigned to them (if your source system allows this). Your mapping of users to sources of truth via a unique identifier should give you a one-for-one match of users with the source of truth (and therefore the business owner). The data you compile might look something like Figure 7-3.

User ID	Name	Unique ID	Source	Access	Bus Owner
JSMITH	John Smith	123456	HRIS	RN	Dir. Nursing
JDOE	Jane Doe	M234567	Med. Staff	MD	Med. Staff
MSMITH	Mary Smith	B345678	Business	BILLER	Business
JJONES	Joseph Jones			RN	
MBO	Michael Bo	C456789	Contr. Med.	PCT	Contract Med Staff

Figure 7-3. Sample data mapping users to sources of truth

In this scenario, you would send John Smith's name to the director of nursing for review, Jane Doe's name to the medical staff office for review, Michael Bo's name to the contract medical staff office for review, and Mary Smith's name to the business office for review. If any of these users have left the organization, the business owner should inform you of this; if all access is appropriate, they should verify this.

But what about Joseph Jones? What do we do with this account? Since the periodic access review process dictates an accounting of all users in the system at a point in time, your job is to figure out who this is. You need to ask yourself some questions. Can you tell what department this user is logging into? Does the access assigned to this user tell you who should validate this access?

You might be tempted to think that the director of nursing would process this request for verification, but there are also nurses who are managed by the contract medical staff office. In this case, sending notification to both of these offices might be your best option. You will need to get creative as you attempt to validate user access.

What if you are not able to find anyone to validate a user account during your periodic access review? One option might be to inactivate the account, and ensure that you are able to capture the correct identity information when the user calls the help desk to have his account activated again. Whatever your process, your goal needs to be a method of positively identifying all users in the system at any point in time, and that you have a system in place for capturing identifying information for anyone who might have slipped through the cracks.

Finally, keep in mind that most systems have built-in controls for inactive user accounts, and these should be turned on and used whenever possible. The inactivity settings that you apply to your users should be based on your organizational security policy. Organizations might choose to implement a less stringent inactivity setting of 90 days for physicians and a more stringent policy of 30 days for all other users. Whatever settings you apply should be consistent, and your process for re-enabling accounts that have been inactivated should be communicated to everyone involved in account creation and maintenance. Inactivity settings are a good way to control for users who might not be easily captured in your deprovisioning workflows.

Role-Based Access Control

One acronym that you should become familiar with, if you aren't already, is RBAC—*role-based access control*. An RBAC system can be deployed for all enterprise systems or per system, depending on your needs. The RBAC approach to security equates a position (*role*) with a defined access configuration, and this access is consistently applied to all users in a given position.

Just as you needed to identify your sources of truth for unique identifiers in user records, you need to identify these sources of truth for your RBAC system. What you need from your sources of truth are the positions, or roles, that you will map to *access*.

It is important to note that roles are generally (though not invariably) more specific than a clinician title such as *RN* or *MD*. Quite often access will be defined by a combination of the department or location where a person works with their job title. An RN who works in the Emergency Department and an RN who works in Surgery both have the same job title, but they have different access needs based on their location.

Suppose your HRIS and medical staff system contain the data shown in Figure 7-4.

Source System	Name	Department	Dept. ID	Job	Job ID
HRIS	Doe, John	Gen. Surg.	12	RN	56
HRIS	Kai, Jen	Gen. Surg.	12	PCT	67
HRIS	Johns, Bo	Emer. Dept.	23	RN	56
HRIS	Min, Jon	Emer. Dept.	23	PCT	67
MED STAFF	Hines, Max	Gen. Surg.	GS	MD	MD
MED STAFF	Tan, Phil	Labor/Deliv.	LD	MD	MD
MED STAFF	Sang, Jill	Gen. Surg.	GS	PA	PA

Figure 7-4. Sample data from HRIS and medical staff system

From the data in Figure 7-4 you can create *position codes* compounded of information about the department and the job, such as those in Figure 7-5.

Source System	Dept./Job	Position Code
HRIS	Gen. Surg. RN	1256
HRIS	Gen. Surg. PCT	1267
HRIS	Emer. Dept. RN	2356
HRIS	Emer. Dept. PCT	2367
MED STAFF	Gen. Surg. MD	GSMD
MED STAFF	Labor/Deliv. MD	LDMD
MED STAFF	Gen. Surg. PA	GSPA

Figure 7-5. Position codes

You have taken the codes for each department and the codes for each job and combined them to create a unique position code for each unique combination of department and job. Furthermore, it doesn't matter if the codes are identical in format. What is important is that your source systems feed your RBAC, and that you can intelligently create a unique position identifier in your RBAC. As new positions are added to your organization, you will be charged with doing a gap analysis of positions in your RBAC against positions in your organization. You will also need to find a meaningful way to account for those users who fall outside of your HRIS, medical staff, and other sources of truth. For instance, if you hire a contract coder in your HIM department, you should record these positions in your RBAC in a logical manner—perhaps HIM for your HIM department and CONCODER for the job called contract coder.

Finally, you will need to assign access to the positions in your organization. This process will take a bit more thought and will require the involvement of stakeholders and decision makers in your organization. The rule of thumb is that the application analysts in charge of building the access for various positions should be the one to specify access appropriate to a given position. Once the *proposed access* is assigned to a position, you will want obtain sign-off from stakeholders in Privacy, Corporate Compliance, Clinical Management (nursing or physician), Health Information Management and other areas as appropriate to the position (for example, Pharmacy Management for pharmacy access).

This step is vital in the completion of your RBAC system since outside auditors will want to assure that access assignments receive organizational input and approval before being deployed in a production environment. We will discuss application design more in the following chapter, but keep in mind that compliance with regulations on privacy and security dictates a segmentation of duties between the "builder" and the approver. This means that your RBAC process should include a decision tracker that documents when organizational privacy and security stakeholders approved access assignment decisions. With this in mind, your final RBAC might look something like Figure 7-6.

Source System	Position Code	Access
HRIS	1256	RN01
HRIS	1267	PCT01
HRIS	2356	RN02
HRIS	2367	PCT02
MED STAFF	GSMD	MD01
MED STAFF	LDMD	MD02
MED STAFF	GSPA	PA01

Figure 7-6. Final RBAC

Finally, don't neglect to consider any other settings for a user account that will affect access. Some medical record systems require that an associated provider record be linked to a user record, and these provider records can contain scores of settings that drive functionality, security. and workflows. Where provider records, or any other similar records, are required, it is often most helpful to create test users in your nonproduction systems with "groupings of access" applied to them (access templates and provider record settings, for instance). A test user-based RBAC might look something like Figure 7-7.

Source System	Position Code	Access
HRIS	1256	TSTRN01
HRIS	1267	TSTPCT01
HRIS	2356	TSTRN02
HRIS	2367	TSTPCT02
MED STAFF	GSMD	TSTPMD01
MED STAFF	LDMD	TSTMD02
MED STAFF	GSPA	TSTPA01

Figure 7-7. Sample user-based RBAC

When your RBAC points to test users, you will be able to capture all of the required security settings for a given position with a single record, and your provisioning can be based on these test users.

With a complete RBAC in place, your last task will be to keep a list of exceptions to the rules. Perhaps a nurse in the operating room has been assigned certain financial responsibilities, and therefore is granted elevated billing access. This exception should be documented with the details of the exception, the date of the approval, and the name of the approving manager. You will certainly need to reference an exception matrix when you are questioned about the unique access that Nurse X has in relation to Nurse Y, who works in the same department.

Enterprise Identity Management Systems

When putting your security program in place, it might be advantageous to work with your technical services or operations team to evaluate and implement an *enterprise identity management system* (IMS). An IMS is typically a software package that works with the existing sources of truth, and creates a master database of all users in the system. While the IMS contains a single record per user in the system, it contains intelligent links to user accounts across systems. An IMS can be designed to facilitate workflows for automated account provisioning based on approved standards (the RBAC), and can also be configured to handle the deprovisioning workflows.

It is not the place of this book to make suggestions about vendors or platforms for an IMS, but it would be wise to consider the place of an IMS in your security program. Many of the processes that we have reviewed to this point are manual, using spreadsheets or desktop database systems, unless automated workflows are developed. Be warned, however, that an IMS system is built on logic and rules, and when you have exceptions to the rules—such as a case manager who has been approved for RN access—an automated system might not work well. There are always programmatic options for complex workflows, but you should be aware of the potential limitations of an enterprise IMS.

The HL7 Interface

Those who have been working in healthcare IT for any length of time will certainly be familiar with the term *HL7 Interface*. "HL7" stands for *Health Level Seven*, which is an international organization devoted to developing and supporting standards that support the exchange of *informatics data*. (*Informatics* is the European name for healthcare IT, and has become a common term of reference worldwide). The "7" in "HL7" refers to the seventh layer of the OSI network model—the application layer. In short, HL7 interfaces can assist in the process of taking data from one system and rendering it in the application layer (the GUI) of your EHR system.

HL7 can be helpful in efforts to build a sustainable support model for user records (and provider records) in an EHR system. If, for instance, the HRIS system contains licensure information, an HL7 interface can be built to regularly update credential related identity information in the EHR. Name changes and other information contained in sources of truth can also be funneled down to the EHR system via an HL7 interface. Look to your vendor for guidance on the availability of identity-related HL7 interfaces. These typically entail a licensing fee, but in the long run they can reduce administrative headaches related to identity.

A Note about Credentials

Access to a system is just part of the identity picture. It is important to note that the data tied to user records (through an associated provider record or otherwise) is an important part of the *legal medical record* (LMR). The EHR system is all about data, and every transaction in an EHR leaves a trail of data in its wake. If someone makes a note in a chart, and the chart shows Jane Doe, RN, as the note author, you had better be sure that this is Jane's proper credential. All of this information associated with a user that is stored in the system has a tendency to become stale if it is not continually reviewed against sources of truth.

A student nurse, for instance, will often graduate and be hired as a full-fledged RN in your organization, and it is important to keep credentials current and her access appropriate to her position. Licensure can lapse, and when it does, it is not appropriate for a user to be documenting in a chart with an expired credential. The only way to ensure that your data stays clean is to set up processes to capture all of the pertinent user information and update the data in your charge appropriately. Often a programmatic approach to updates is preferred because it is less prone to error and decreases the workload of the administrative staff. However, it is never appropriate to provision user accounts without a plan to maintain them over time. If you are charged with ensuring that access and identity are correct, then update your processes accordingly and confirm that they are being followed.

Know Your Enemies

As we noted at the beginning of this chapter, the process of managing the identity of users in your system will help you create a secure environment for your patients. Know yourself, and you will know your enemies. If you know all of your own people, you can treat the "rest" as suspect and control them accordingly. If you can't identify your own users, then your risk levels are high and you do a disservice to customers who rely on you to treat their private information with utmost care.

Application Design

Maximum Efficiency or Minimum Necessary?

Lord Darlington: ... I can resist everything except temptation.
Lady Windermere: You have the modern affectation of weakness.

—Oscar Wilde, *Lady Windermere's Fan*

It wasn't long before questions started to pour in: "Why in the world does our pastoral care staff have the ability to discontinue medications?" "Why do our technicians have the ability to edit cancer protocols?"

The short response to these probing questions was, "We'll address that right away; it's obviously not correct." But the underlying problem was one that had to be addressed—if there were problems in these two areas, there were certainly problems in other areas as well, and a systematic approach to access and application design would need to be employed to address the issue.

But what happened in the first place?

Building Blocks

It is important to understand that an EMR system is built for certain clinical workflows that are primary—an ambulatory physician or a nurse, for instance. When functionality is extended to additional types of users or roles, the application vendor will often start with what works (or what already exists) and build on that.

Recurring to the chapter setup about the pastoral care user—the "chaplain" in a medical system—can you hazard a guess about the starting point that led to the chaplain's access permitting him to discontinue medications?

The most logical guess is that the inappropriate privilege was entailed by the granting of clinical documentation user status to allow the chaplain to document charts in an EMR system. (Some chaplains in some organizations are still given only a simple census report with no documentation abilities, but such users are increasingly being integrated as members of the care team and therefore require access to document in the chart.)

■ **Note**   Each EMR vendor's application is different, but the principles of solid application security build remain the same—what a user in a given role has access to should be appropriate to the position. It is the application security analyst's job to ensure that it the application is built securely; the job of leadership is to validate that the analyst has built what is appropriate for a given position.

The EMR vendor or the application analyst who built the pastoral care access might have used the nurse role as a starting point. But when one begins with existing "build" or security, one is obliged to make sure that only the rights appropriate to the new position remain. This task can be a tedious and time-consuming, yet it is key to the successful deployment of a secure EMR.

The same goes for a technician. Knowing what the technician in question should be able to do, you might for the sake of efficiency scour the system to find an analogous user that fits the profile and duplicate it. But absent due diligence, you court the danger of entraining inappropriate features of the starting point.

The work to ensure that access is role-appropriate is important, and the analysis that goes into this is a vital part of any EMR deployment. Be certain that you have the right people in these analyst positions!

What's in a Name?

Juliet said of Romeo, "What's in a name? That which we call a rose by any other name would smell as sweet." The essence of a person is not in his name, for if you changed his name to anything else, he would still be, in essence, who and what he was before.

I argue that the person charged with "application build," "application security," "application design," or whatever you might choose to call it will be, in essence, your application security analyst. Regardless of the title that he bears, or what he might feel his strengths are, his responsibilities are clear and will not change—**to ensure the integrity and security of the application that you are deploying to your customers.**

The word *analyst* cannot be emphasized enough! Perhaps your application security analyst, or "security analyst" (that's what we'll call this employee in this chapter, and from here on out, regardless of the title that this employee might bear), was previously a nurse or a technician in your organization before taking a job on your IT staff.

The former nurse is charged with building out the EMR for other nurses, perhaps, and maybe this new security analyst feels that the value they bring to the team is in the comprehension of clinical workflows, not in the complex, inner workings of the software you are deploying.

What you must communicate to your security analyst quickly and clearly is that although the experience they bring from their previous job might be an asset (potentially a **huge** asset), their new job as a security analyst requires them to take that knowledge and convey that to the technical world in which they now live. They are no longer a clinician, but a clinical informaticist.

The analyst's job, by definition, requires mastery of a process that takes information gathered in exploratory and validation sessions and conveys it to a properly designed application. Workflows translated into a properly functioning application can only happen with good analysis, and good analysis will lead to a solid understanding of what is contextually appropriate for a given user and what is inappropriate.

At the most basic level, the security analyst deploys what is required to perform a job, and removes those functions and tools that are inappropriate to a given position.

Brass Tacks

Interviewing techniques aside (each organization has its own theories and strategies about how to hire the best and brightest, and behavior-based interviews seem to be all the rage right now), it is obvious that hiring the wrong employee not only can be very costly but can impact your ability to produce the results that are expected from your team.

Some vendors will strongly encourage you to staff your implementation team from within your organization, using existing clinical and technical staff to build the EMR for the organization; the merits of this approach are rather straightforward. Retention of longtime employees after implementation is more likely, and when you pull from a workforce that already knows the workflows and the corporate ethos, the learning curve can be reduced significantly.

But think long and hard about the type of people who will work side by side for many hours each day, for what will turn into very long days toward the end of your project. Consider the fact that a personable nurse who has earned merit promotions consistently throughout a long career might not be the right person to serve as an analyst on the EMR implementation team.

Just because a beloved, efficient, and highly respected technician from the oncology department wants to take a position as an analyst on the cancer application team does not ensure that this individual will serve well as a security analyst.

The High Cost of a Bad Hire

The reality of the situation is that once a hiring manager places an analyst on a team, there are several factors that will make it unlikely that the person will leave the team, even if the he or she turns out to be no analyst at all (a nonanalyst by any other name, even if an "analyst" in title, is still not an analyst!).

First, there is the fact that it is difficult to explain to leadership that you didn't hire the right person for the job after all. The question that might come back at you is, "Why didn't this come out in the interview?"

A host of other factors enter the equation, such as the potential that terminating an employee might result in the loss of that position from the team—some managers would rather have that less than productive member on their team than to risk losing a full-time employee that they fought hard to "earn."

Finally, when an employee leaves an organization, it is not cheap! It is generally accepted that the cost to replace an employee—including recruitment costs, relocation expenses, training, productivity loss during transition, and so on—is roughly 75 percent of their annual salary.

A nonproductive analyst being paid $70,000 is expensive, and the cost to replace the analyst with another employee is also not cheap (Figure 8-1). At $52,000, it is certainly better to be sure that you have the right person for the job up front!

Termination and rehiring of an analyst at a cost of 75% of their annual salary ...

Nonanalyst @ $70K

Cost to Replace = $52,500

Figure 8-1. Nonanalyst replacement costs

The Core Skills

This isn't a human resources manual—you can certainly find plenty of assistance on interviewing techniques and such elsewhere—but the following core skills should be essential in all of your analyst hires. Certainly your security analysts should have these skills to ensure the integrity of your application.

1. **Communication skills.** While a great communicator alone, without good technical skills, might not make a good analyst, a good analyst has to be able to bridge the gap between the data and the end-users/management. Be sure you have someone who can hold their own with a dictionary. I have seen it suggested that it is wise to have your job candidates wait for 10–15 minutes near your current employees and observe how they engage with them during this unscripted time.

2. **Clinical proficiency.** Although it isn't necessary to know the intricacies of hemodialysis and toxicology, it is important to have a solid working knowledge of the clinical realm, knowing the differences between different clinical roles and practice areas.

3. **Data prowess.** I cannot overstate how important it is for an analyst to be able to confront head on the numbers and information (data) that will drive the functionality of the application. If the analyst cannot take large amounts of data from multiple sources and "make sense" of it by manipulating it in a meaningful way, then you will face challenges. An analyst doesn't always need to have the answers at his fingertips, but he must be able to find the answers in short order. I propose that any interview for an analyst position should be technical to some extent. Have your candidates demonstrate some real problem-solving skills with numbers and information before you hire them, expecting them to do the same!

4. **Detail-oriented.** All of these skills or strengths are possibly irrelevant if the analyst is unable to hone in on what is important to the task at hand. Finding out if your candidate is detail-oriented can be as simple as asking two questions, (a) "When were you able to solve a problem recently by keying in on the details during a project?" and (b) "When did you suffer the effects of poor planning and attention to detail?"

Arguments, Arguments, Arguments

So, you have hired your team, or perhaps you have inherited your team. You need to begin the work of evaluating what you have to work with. As you begin the process of discovery (and, yes, you *must* work through the process of reviewing the application build for propriety), you will perhaps run into several different breeds of application analysts who will argue that the things you are discovering as "inappropriate" actually need to stay there. I break these application analysts down into two camps; your job will be to lead them out of the dark side.

The Don't-Touch It-You'll-Break-It Analyst

In every organization there seems to be at least one analyst (in my experience there are many!) who will look at the items you point out as inappropriate build and respond with something to the effect of the following argument: "I understand that you don't like the fact that this button is there for these users, but things work the way that they are built now, and if we start to mess with things, there is a good chance they will break."

In other words, they saw exactly what you saw, and they know that the application is not built properly, but they aren't confident enough in their abilities to fix it and ensure that it will still work properly. They hear you but want to leave well enough alone and keep it just like it is.

The excuses that you will be given about why the change is not practical will vary (and the analyst certainly won't be so blunt as to admit that ineptitude is the true underlying reason that the "bad build" remains intact), but you can count on the fact that the "Don't touch it; you'll break it" analyst lurks out there in most organizations, waiting to justify inaction at all costs.

You can see why this approach is problematic.

The More-Access-Is-Better Analyst

More often you will find the analyst who will take your feedback about access that might not seem appropriate and respond with a variation on a theme of the following argument: "Yes, I understand that you don't think it's appropriate for these users to have access to this activity, but we have given this activity to all of our users. Managers are supposed to train their users how to use the system appropriately. If I start taking buttons away from users as you are asking me to do, I am going to need to start maintaining many more iterations of access for my users, and I don't think that is a good approach. More access, and fewer variations, is better."

The problems with this approach are layered, but at the core is the flawed assumption that a single, broadly designed access paradigm for multiple types of users is a viable option for your users.

Think about it: If this approach was valid, a single "view" into the EMR system that encompassed everyone from physicians to housekeeping (and everyone in between) would be sufficient. Every button and every menu would work to accomplish a task, but you would instruct users to simply "Click on only those items that are applicable and appropriate to your job!"

Oh, the chaos that would ensue—not to mention the lawsuits!

The Middle Way

There is certainly are potential problems when you start to narrowly define access based on role or position in an organization. You can suddenly find that people are unable to perform a job that they should be able to perform according to their credentials.

Say, for instance, you build access for your *emergency department* (ED) nurses, and in this access is a "snapshot view" of all ED patients that should truly be viewed by nurses in the ED only. When this tool is deployed, narrowly, to a subset of nurses that work in the ED, your "build" restriction works as planned.

But what happens when a nurse who is typically assigned to the Critical Care Department is called to cover a shift in the ED? If you have so narrowly restricted your build that nurses in other parts of the organization don't have access to these ED-specific tools when they are needed, then you have created deficiencies in productivity that really weren't necessary. The ED snapshot view is something that, practically speaking, all of your nurses should be able to access when they are working in the ED.

With this in mind, you can build your application in a way such that all appropriate functionality within a **given discipline** is incorporated into standards of access per discipline.

Therefore, all appropriate tools for nurses can be deployed to a standard access for all nurses. The same would be true for all nurse practitioners, nurse anesthetists, and nursing assistants.

You can be sure that access appropriate to a nurse anesthetist would probably be inappropriate to deploy to a nursing assistant, and this is where we need to be concerned in the realm of application security. Not only are workflows different, but patient safety issues abound when someone is technologically allowed to do something that, by license and training, they are not permitted to do.

Minimum Necessary

Built into the HIPAA Privacy Rule is some language that anticipates the problems that would arise if a member of the environmental services staff was able to order narcotics, or if a member of the patient transport team was able to see sensitive lab results (both things should never be able to happen).

The HIPAA Privacy Rule includes what is called the *minimum necessary standard*, which generally states that any PHI provided to employees of a healthcare organization must be appropriate to their job and in keeping with adopted internal policies.

The language of the standard is deliberately broad so as to not place an undue burden on healthcare providers, but there is a clear expectation that some thought will be given to how access to patient data is deployed. Furthermore, the straightforward name of the standard implies that access to PHI will be based on a principle of what is the "minimum necessary" to do a given job in related to patient care.

The precise language is: "A covered entity must make reasonable efforts to limit protected health information to the minimum necessary to accomplish the intended purpose of the use, disclosure or request" (§ 164.528(b)).

It is all fine and good if an organization, by policy, provides EMR access to all of its administrative assistants so that they can run a standard report or check on the admission status of a patient, but you can be sure that such an approach to access does not comply with the HIPAA minimum necessary standard.

The question to ask is, "What report, or reports, do the administrative assistants need access to?" Then, appropriate access can be built for this group of users.

It is certainly easy to look at the request for access, and say, "Well, our basic chart view access has the information that the administrative assistants will need, let's give that to them!" Beware of this slippery slope!

Likewise, when you are building access for the various users in your organization, you need to look at the access that has been granted to them and review the propriety of the access. Go ahead—log in as a test user with that new access and take a look at the button and menus that the user will have! Are they contextually appropriate?

■ **Note** Just as it is important to understand regulations such as the HIPAA Privacy Rule, knowing the nuances of its parts, such as the **minimum necessary standard**, will be important as you engage with leadership and technical staff on the matter of application security.

It is not enough to say, "This new role needs to be able to document in the chart and administer medications. Our RN role can do that—I'll copy the RN access for this new position." Wait a minute! What about all of the other things that an RN can do by license that are entirely inappropriate for this new position that you are charged with building? Has this access been removed?

Again, keep access consistent and broad within a given domain or discipline—there really shouldn't be too many iterations of RN access. Keep it simple there. But be careful to avoid the pitfalls of sloppy build when it comes to different roles. Always keep the mantra *minimum necessary* in the back of your mind, and think about how you have complied with this standard.

The federal government hasn't explicitly spelled out what this will look like in each organization, but there is an expectation that it will be thoughtfully applied for the sake of patient privacy and regulatory compliance.

Let the builder beware! Follow the *middle way* and build broadly for ease of access within a discipline while keeping strong **fences around your job titles.**

A Dose of Liberality

For all of this talk about *minimum necessary* and *building fences*, it is important to reiterate that usability should never pointlessly suffer in the name of security.

It is important that you always build your application with a view to usability. When you are tempted to place a restriction on a user, or a group of users, ask the question: "Am I considering this restriction because this user could never perform this function in their position/with their credentials?" If the answer is yes, then by all means push forward with your good build.

Note   Involve your security stakeholders in the process of defining the parameters of acceptable practice for various disciplines in your organization.

If you are placing restrictive build on a user type to prevent something that could conceivably be permitted in this role, then reconsider these restrictions. This is the type of behavior that should be regulated by policy.

You will sometimes be presented with concerns from managers or directors who want you to limit access to certain functions because a user (or users) in the organization cannot seem to follow proper protocol. This is an occasion to push back and ask that the users be managed rather than putting administratively complex build into a system that will likely cause problems for other users down the road.

Just because you can limit or control something in the application does not necessarily mean that you should. Remember that opening up access to all features and functions that are appropriate and reasonable to a given license/ position will lead to maximum productivity while maintaining the integrity of your system.

A Note about Sensitive Information

It is inevitable in the course of an EMR implementation that the topic of *sensitive information* will arise. This umbrella term encompasses data such as Social Security numbers and psychiatric notes.

It is imperative that an organizational policy for the treatment of sensitive information is documented and communicated clearly to all of your application security analysts. Some of the questions you will need to answer include, but are not limited to:

- Who will have access to the full Social Security number of patients? Will anyone outside of the Health Information Management (HIM) Office have access to this? How will you enforce this policy?

- How will you control printing of sensitive information? Who will be allowed to print information, and what types of information can be printed? What is your organizational policy concerning the handling and disposal of printed PHI?

- Who will have access to psychiatric treatment data? Will psychotherapy notes be treated differently from notes in the rest of the chart? How will you control access to psychiatric treatment data? Will psychiatric departments be browsable and visible to anyone in the organization? How will you audit this information?

- How will you handle VIP and celebrity patient charts? Will these be restricted from view by your user base, or will they be visible as any other chart?

Although the information in a patient chart is by nature sensitive and worthy of all protective measures we can bring to the table, the sampling of sensitive issues related to the patient chart that extend beyond issues of diagnosis, treatment, and care highlight the complexities presented to the application analyst.

A Psychiatric Case in Point

In an inpatient setting, it is common to have a list of units or floors that can be browsed for clinicians to find their patients. When these lists are open to all, without restriction, and sensitive units such as behavioral health are included, your user base has access to information that is much more tempting to the prying eyes of curious onlookers.

Sure, you should expect your employees to respect the privacy of all of your patients, and those in your behavioral health units are no exception.

Let's look at some possible scenarios.

A technician in your organization comes home from work one evening to find an ambulance at his neighbor's house, and upon speaking with the family, he finds that a child in the home suffered a serious fracture and was being taken to the hospital where he would likely be admitted for several days.

The technician could easily (against policy) look at the patient chart to see how the child is doing, but he is more likely to check with the neighbor when he gets home from work the next day, "How is Billy doing? Is his leg healing well?"

Consider another scenario where the same technician gets word through the neighborhood rumor mill that another neighbor attempted suicide, nearly died, and was admitted to the behavioral health hospital after being stabilized in the emergency department.

In this case, the technician likewise has no business accessing the patient chart of the neighbor who he suspects was admitted to the behavioral health hospital, but the temptation, even for a generally honest employee, is immense in this situation.

What if the employee doesn't access the chart, but simply looks at the list of patients in the behavioral health unit to see if the neighbor was indeed admitted, confirming the rumor?

In the latter case, where the chart wasn't accessed, an audit event would probably not be triggered, but the technician would be armed with enough information to be dangerous. "Yes, I saw Bill's name on the list of patients in the behavioral health hospital, so the rumor must be true!"

The fiduciary responsibility of the organization toward those with particularly sensitive information in the chart is therefore greater than it is in the case of the general patient population (and this responsibility is not small in regard to the "normal" patient!). The minimum necessary standard, which is an expectation of the HIPAA Privacy Rule, kicks into overdrive when it comes to sensitive data, and it is vital that this is considered at length when the EMR is built.

Consider, here, who has access to browse behavioral health units and ensure that only those who should have access do. Perhaps this would be your credentialed providers with a specialty of behavioral health. There are a host of ways to control access to sensitive information, and it is the job of the security analyst to evaluate the options and assist the organization in deploying a solution that encourages productive workflows while protecting a patient's reasonable expectation of privacy.

A Holistic Approach

However your organization decides to handle its sensitive information, it is vital that your team of security analysts understands what is at stake and that the build is consistent across applications.

It is wonderful if you decide that only users with a listed specialty of behavioral health will be able to see psychotherapy notes, but if you have no mechanism to control who is granted that specialty, then your control is weak.

Likewise, if you control access to the full Social Security number through a programming mechanism, but one application analyst does not follow your policy on applying that security, then your controls are likewise useless (or, at the very least, inconsistent).

Note In 2013, a healthcare system employee was fired for accessing patient charts and then the IRS website to file fraudulent tax returns with information from the patient charts (which included name, address, date of birth, and Social Security number). This case illustrates the importance of not only auditing the use of the EMR by employees but limiting who has access to sensitive information. If one key element in the chart, the Social Security number, had been blocked, these cases of fraud might have been prevented.

Be sure to document your policies on the handling of sensitive information, thoughtfully consider the minimum necessary standard, and follow through with checks so that the controls actually work. Your customers deserve nothing less than extreme diligence in this domain!

What Does This Look like?

A discussion about application security is a good starting point, but it is helpful to consider some examples of what this might look like to your analysts and end users.

First, it would be impractical to consider every iteration of access, because the EMR in the twenty-first century is composed of the chart, navigators, elements of revenue cycle applications, and more. There is no way to comprehensively address the possible application build issues that a security analyst might face (not to mention the fact that each EMR system is unique). With these caveats in mind, the following mock EMR system presents a few of the common issues that security analysts and medical systems should be aware of and seek to address as they build out a secure EMR. We'll be looking at access for a generic clinical user.

Know Your EMR

As you can see in Figure 8-2, there is a lot going on when a user logs into the EMR. It is important to understand the various elements that are presented in the application when a user logs in, to know what is appropriate to each role, and what function each element performs.

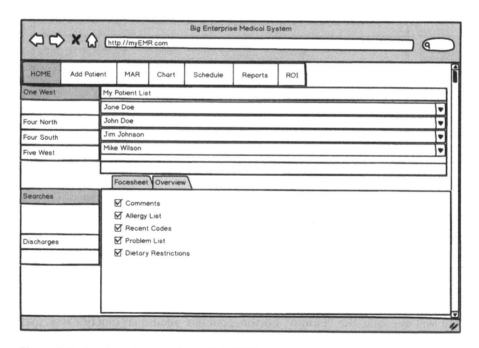

Figure 8-2. Sample main screen for a clinical EMR user

Notice below that various common elements of the EMR are available to the user, including a list of units, the Facesheet, the MAR (Medical Administration Record), the Chart, the Schedule, Reports and more.

Clicking Through

It would be nice if you could log in to the EMR and see if access was appropriate at first glance, but in practice it is essential to click through the application to understand what has been configured and deployed to your various users. In Figure 8-3, you have opened the Chart view.

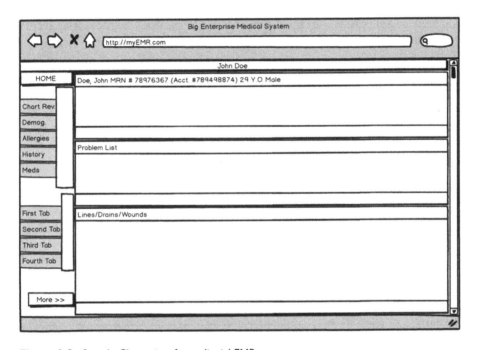

Figure 8-3. Sample Chart view for a clincial EMR user

When you open the chart, a series of tabs display for the user. These may be different for your various clinical users, depending on their roles. Review what is deployed in the Chart view, and note whether the functionality, as deployed, seems appropriate to your user.

As you continue clicking through the application (Figure 8-4), note the functionality behind the different menus and buttons. In the case that follows, you will see that the "Home" button contains additional functionality that might or might not be appropriate for the clinical user we are reviewing.

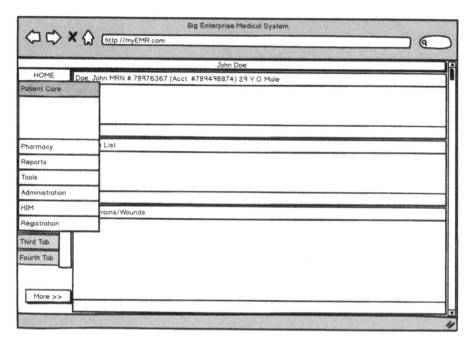

Figure 8-4. Click-through exploration of clinical EMR user

In this case, you would look at the access behind each menu, but you would key in on the Pharmacy menu (this might not be necessary for a clinical user) and the Administration menu.

When you see something that is out of place, such as the Pharmacy menu in Figure 8-4, you will want to explore what is driving this. Think back to the discussion of the origins of access for many of the users—often access from another area is "copied" as a starting point, but security that isn't desirable or necessary often gets dragged into the new access. In this case, looking at the backend build for Pharmacy-related security will probably lead to the source of this menu. If it isn't needed for this user, then remove it.

Now look at the Administration menu to see what is there. In Figure 8-5, the Administration menu contains an item that would certainly be unnecessary, and dangerous, for a clinical user. The Security Administration menu would allow manipulation of user records in the system, including changing other users' passwords!

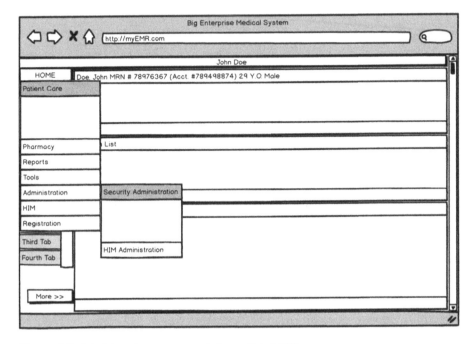

Figure 8-5. Administration menu sample for a clinical EMR user

This might seem absurd to think that a clinical user, such as a nurse or a patient care technician, would have access to change user passwords in the system, but this is just the sort of sloppy build that will need to be reviewed in the process of an EMR deployment.

Remnants of inappropriate access often make their way into standard security build for users of all sorts. Without a careful eye for these sorts of anomalies, dangerous build errors such as these will find their way into the production environment, and you might only find out about them after it's too late!

Again, many of these problems will only be discovered with a click through review of access, which might seem tedious and time-consuming but is necessary to ensure that you don't let errors like this slip through the cracks.

Finally, don't leave any stone unturned in the process of reviewing access. In Figure 8-6, the More button is expanded, exposing the presence of the Cancer Protocol Administration tool.

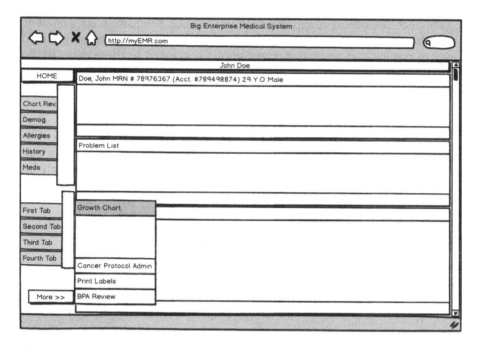

Figure 8-6. The More activity reveals additional inappropriate tools

The presence of such obscure menus might evade many users (and most users intent on doing their jobs would never stumble across this), but such tools in the hand of a curious employee with too much free time on a slow shift could lead to patient safety issues and a lawsuit.

Don't ever assume that because access generally looks good on logging into the system that all is built appropriately. It is vital that a process be put in place to review the build of your security analysts.

Build, Review, Approve (Repeat)

Hopefully, you will find that most of your security analysts will build out their applications with the utmost diligence, and atrocious examples such as those listed here will not be an issue for your organization. It is nonetheless critical to establish a review mechanism once the access is built.

The final step after access is reviewed is to have your security stakeholders approve the access as built, and then document that approval where it can be referenced if there is ever a question about that access in the future.

Finally, once the access is approved for use in your production environment, your change control mechanisms (and your change review board) should work to ensure that no unauthorized access is granted to these users in the future.

Don't Let Them Drag You Down

When all is said and done, you will have competing factions who argue that your security interests are competing with usability and will ultimately be a drag on productivity. Don't buy into that for a second—nothing could be further from the truth.

The goal of a secure EMR does *not* have to compete with goals of usability. You can have your cake and eat it, too (contrary to popular belief!).

The bottom line is that a secure, efficient EMR has to be built well, and that takes work. This is the kind of work that can only be accomplished through complex analysis and build. Whether your organization has done its diligence in hiring the kind of people who can accomplish this task is another matter.

Most bright individuals can rise to the occasion if they are held to task and given clear deliverables. Your security analysts will not be able to build a secure EMR if the expectations placed on them are ambiguous, or if they receive competing messages from different parts of the organization. This is where executive support for your security initiatives and goals is vital—when the top echelon understands what you hope to accomplish with a secure EMR, and this is communicated throughout the ranks, your job is much easier, and your EMR will indeed be secure.

Further Reading

HHS and HIPAA, "Minimum Necessary Standard," http://www.hhs.gov/ocr/privacy/hipaa/understanding/coveredentities/minimumneces-sary.pdf (accessed January 23, 2014).

HHS "General Rules for Disclosure of PHI", CFR-2010-title45-vol1-sec164-502, http://www.gpo.gov/fdsys/pkg/CFR-2010-title45-vol1/pdf/CFR-2010-title45-vol1-sec164-502.pdf (accessed February 12, 2014).

Goldman, Jeff, "Holy Cross Hospital Acknowledges Insider Breach," October 1, 2013, http://www.esecurityplanet.com/network-security/holy-cross-hospital-acknowledges-insider-breach.html (accessed February 26, 2014).

Access Validation Process

An Approach to Validating Access and Receiving Stakeholder Signoff

When you get to the point of validating access for your user types or roles, it is helpful to have a process in place that can be repeated for each of your *templates* (in Epic speak), *profiles* (in Meditech speak), or whatever role-based standards of access you might need your stakeholders to sign off on.

The following framework provides a general process that can be used in the process of assuring that you aren't putting standards of access into production without appropriate approval.

Validation Groupings

Before you begin the process of seeking approval, you need to gather your test users, or types of access into logical groupings. Put these into a spreadsheet, and organize them in a way that makes the most sense to you (Figure 9-1). Be sure to include only as many roles or user types as you will be able to review in a given session in your logical groupings.

User Login	User Name	Review Week
INTERPRETER	INTERPRETER, NH	1
IPHEALART	INPATIENT, HEALING ART	1
SC	INPATIENT, SPIRITUAL CARE	1
IPRT	PRACTITIONER, RESPIRATORY CARE	2
IPRTSUP	INPATIENT, RT SUPERVISOR	2
NEUROTECH	NEUROLOGY, TECHNOLOGIST	2
IPRD	INPATIENT, NUTRITION	3
IPRECT	THERAPIST, RECREATIONAL	3
OT	THERAPIST, OCCUPATIONAL	3
PT	PHYSICAL, THERAPIST	3

Figure 9-1. Sample validation groupings

Organize a Schedule

When you are ready to organize a schedule, you need to consider many more elements than a title, date and attendees on a shared resource such as Exchange or Groupwise.

In my experience, you will need at least 90 to 120 minutes per validation session. Much less time, and you will be rushed, much more time, and your stakeholders will become weary of the process. Also, you will likely be able to schedule a validation session, maybe two, in a week. If you schedule two in a week, you will probably not want to repeat this pattern the next week—remember, your stakeholders are, by nature, high profile employees in your organization, and there are many demands on their time.

Now start to do the math—you might have 60, 80 or 150 different types of access to approve with a new implementation—it is going to take you months of well orchestrated meetings to review all of that access.

If you have grouped the access types together well, you might need three weeks to review the access for your surgical staff, 5 weeks for your clinical staff, 2–3 weeks for your orders related staff, and so on.

Look at your groupings, and begin to visually space out your types of access on the calendar so that your stakeholders and subject matter experts can take a breather between these often grueling sessions. If you have a week or two when you have a lot of clinical applications to review, then put a week or two of revenue cycle applications on the docket before diving back into the process with the same subject matter experts.

I find that keeping the calendar master schedule in Excel affords the most flexibility (Figure 9-2). You can always create iCal or Exchange meeting requests to go along with the master schedule.

MON	TUE	WED	THU	FRI		Date	Templates
7	8	9	Clindoc 1-2:30 Bus, Ctr.	11	NOV	10-Nov	Interpeter, Healing Arts, Spiritual Care, Central Distribution
14	15	16	Clindoc- CPOM	18		17-Nov	Resp Care Practicioner, RT Supervisor, Neurology Technologist.
21	22	23	24	25		23-Nov	
28	29	CANCELLED: RESCHEDULE REQUIRED HB/CAD	1	2	DEC	30-Nov	THBINS, THBBAP, THBFINMGMT, THBPAT, THBREFUND, THBSP, THBADM-TESFRONTDESK
							HIM: RESCHEDULE: HIMCODER, HIMCODMGR, HIMCORRECT, HIMDEFAN, HIMDIRECTOR, HIMYMGR

Figure 9-2. Sample master schedule

Always include the location, the primary, the application presenter in the validation session, and the time when you will be meeting. Remember that these sessions are coordinated by someone with a vested interest in privacy and security, but the application security analysts must own the presentation of the application build that they have completed, so they have to be on the hook to present at each of these sessions.

Finally—don't invite too many people to these meetings. You'll find that lots of people are interested in the work that you are doing, but limit attendance to the people that are required to accomplish the work. Too many cooks in the kitchen can spoil the meal.

The Validation Session

You need to create a slide deck that will serve as a template for your security analysts to use in each session—if you don't do this, then there won't be a consistency in the presentation, and your stakeholders will be frustrated by the inconsistency.

In your slide deck, you should include the following slides:

- **Introduction Slide:** This slide should include the names of all templates/profiles/test users that your analyst will be presenting for validation—the list should cover as many users as you can reasonably expect to cover in the 90–120 minutes allotted. Include a spot for the analyst's name and the date of the presentation for historical reference.

- **A "Big Picture" Slide:** This slide should provide your users with a visual summary of how security fits together in your EMR. The various components that make up what a user can see and do in the EMR are difficult to grasp for many nontechnical people, and a visual diagram and explanation of this is helpful. After your stakeholders have been to 3 or 4 sessions, they will not need to see this, but your SME's who are coming to a session for the first time will need to see this at the beginning of each session.

- **Position Designation Slide:** This slide will be a general breakdown of the positions in your organization that will receive the access you are discussion. The access grid from Chapter 7 on Identity and Access Management will be helpful at this point. Show your managers how you will be applying access to your end users by department and job title, and provide them the names of some of their employees who fit into these positions.

- **Access/Role Summary Slides:** You will have a slide for each one of your templates/profiles/roles, and this slide will show your stakeholders and SME's, at a glance, the general functionality of the access. This should be in narrative form.

- **Access/Role Detail Slide:** This slide should give the stakeholders and SME's a little more detail about the access you intend to provide the end users, with specifics about any advanced access (administrative type) that will be provided. Think "Chart Review, Schedule, Medication, Allergies, Patient Lists, Order Entry, Care Plans, etc."

- **Click-Through Slide:** Finally, finish out your slide deck with a slide that says, "And now for the access Click-Through/Walk-Through." In this step your users should be prepared to explore the menu structure and work-flows with the stakeholders and SME's, stop to address concerns vocalized (and document those in a problem list) and to track and record build change requests. Avoid stopping to address matters of engineering or optimization at this point as you are merely addressing access and security in this phase.

The Change Log

When you have finished your security validation session, you will need to be sure that all of the input you have received in the session is documented for follow-up.

It is most helpful if you keep all of your validation session materials, including presentation materials, calendar and change log, in a single location such as a network file share or SharePoint server directory. Just be sure you keep track of the feedback from your stakeholders, and follow up to assure that your security analysts have accommodated the build changes that are required to make your application secure. Figure 9-3 is a sample of a tracking mechanism for requested changes, and actions taken toward a remedy.

Application	Template / User	Issue	Priority R/Y/G	Addressed/Resolved? (description)
Clindoc	Central Distribution	Remove patient summary when clicking on chart.		Resolved
Clindoc	Central Distribution	Remove Diagnosis column on Unit Census (or remove census entirely)?		Resolved- Replaced Unit Census with Info Census that does not have diagnosis colu

Figure 9-3. Sample tracking of stakeholder feedback

Update the Schedule

As you proceed through the validation process, be sure that you update your schedule every step along the way. You will certainly have a session or two cancelled, and as your project picks up steam, usually toward a Go Live, you will find that scheduling time with your stakeholders becomes increasingly more difficult.

Be sure you mark your master schedule when a session is complete, or when adjustments to a schedule are necessary. If you only cover a portion of what you intended to cover in one session, be sure to figure out where that can logically fit down the road, or if another session needs to be scheduled.

Approval of Access

These validation sessions are your formal process of approving standards of access in your organization. You will want to have thorough documentation of what you accomplished, and approved, in each session. To this end, be sure that you keep a sign-in sheet at each session, and store this in the directory where the rest of your validation materials are kept. This will be the data that your external auditors will want to see when you have to justify why you gave certain users access down the road.

Finally, your formal matrix of access (your RBAC), should include a note indicating the date that access was approved. If you have mapped, for instance, Infection Control Nurse to access that you call RN2, then you should have a column called "Validated Date," where you can indicate the date of your validation session. You might even code the validation sessions with their own IDs for easy cross-reference in the future.

Takeaways

1. Invite your stakeholders and subject matter experts to these meetings, but keep the meetings as small as possible.

2. Your directors of compliance, nursing and HIM will be your consistent attendees at most of these meetings (or, at least this should be the case).

3. The pace of these sessions will quicken as people become familiar with what certain functions are, and routine questions don't need to be answered week after week.

Organization of Validation Materials

As noted, be sure to keep your validation materials well organized for future reference, and, at the very least, assure that you have the following items in a discreet folder for each session:

- **Meeting Minutes:** In addition to your change log, be sure to have someone (not the presenter) take minutes during the meeting, and file these for reference. There will inevitably be a point in time when you are going back to make a requested change, but the context for the change is not there.

- **Scanned List of Attendee Signatures:** Don't just have a typed list of attendees, but have a sign-in sheet at validation that the attendees were there. Check-boxes next to names or a typed name can always be refuted later. A signature is harder to refute down the road.

- **Presentation Materials:** The Power Point (or other) presentation materials that were used to demonstrate access to those in attendance.

New Job Codes / Roles

Regarding new job codes that are created after validation, you will need a process to handle these, adding them into your RBAC and access matrix as approved.

- These will evolve quickly during late build/testing and after Go-Lives.

- These are not practical to evaluate and authorize as new templates are built, but an accurate record of what has been built since application validation should be maintained.

- This might change as build settles/subsides and access is standardized.

- Will maintain a list of job codes with either a template specified, or "No Access"

- Security / application teams should review these Positions w/ no access specified, and list as "Access" or "No Access."

Plan: Quarterly review with stakeholders to review non-validated templates assigned to roles or job codes. Should summarize activities in new templates (roles) for quick review, and demo/review any access that the Stakeholders have questions about.

Audit

Three are two types of access audits you will need to perform during your maintenance phase:

- IT / Major Build Changes: IT Security should own this type of auditing which includes Security Settings changes and User Role setting changes (in some cases failed access attempts).

- Clinical and Rev. Cycle: Includes most other areas already reviewed. This job needs to reside in a department that understands clinical workflows such as compliance or HIM.

There is a tendency to think that the security team should be responsible for all auditing functions within the EMR. As noted above, auditing things such as role changes, access changes and build changes can certainly reside within your security team.

As for functions such as whether or not actions taken within the EMR by certain individuals are appropriate, such as viewing medications, looking at notes and so forth, these are actions that only someone with an eye for the types of activities that are appropriate by job type will be able to spot as suspicious.

So, if your EMR vendor has canned reports or audit logs that can be run and reviewed, avoid at all costs having your security team own these processes. This is a function of your compliance, HIM, or other appropriate role—not your IT department.

Periodic Access Review

If you have successfully implemented an RBAC system in your organization, the next step will be to periodically assure that the access being used in your organization is consistent with what was approved.

- If you can correlate Epic access to your HRIS system, you can validate that access is appropriate.

- For those users outside of HRIS systems, linking access to a responsible manager will enable you to review who has access, and receive periodic sign-off from responsible managers.

Troubleshooting and Support

Having reviewed the process of validating access, where did the onus lie in building, demonstrating and fixing access? On each application analyst and the team supporting the application, not on the security team. The security office facilitates secure build and compliance with regulations, but the job of assuring that end-users can do what they need to do, and not more, lies with the application analysts, not your security office.

It is tempting to push security issues—such as, "My button for this is gone," or, "I can't get to that"—off on the team with security in its name, but the proper locus for these issues should fall with the analysts who built that access in the first place. When the troubleshooting is complete, and a change needs to be applied, perhaps it is the security analyst that needs to make the final change—segmentation of duties is always a good idea.

Assuring that you have a well oiled security machine in place is often as simple as making sure that everyone understands their proper role in the system.

Make sure that your helpdesk knows how to triage support calls properly—nothing frustrates an end-user more than to call the helpdesk with an issues only to be passed to someone who tells you he can't help you either.

Lather, Rinse, Repeat

Remember, once you validate access, you need to keep the process going. Transition your weekly validation meetings into a standing committee that will meet quarterly, if only to review a handful of requests of build changes. Get approval from leadership for the processes that you put in place once you are live with your EMR, and assure that you have record of this to show your auditors when they come knocking. Finally, know that if you are diligent about your access standards, and you keep good records, you will be able to sleep well at night—at least on this front.

Physical and Environmental Safeguards

Security beyond the Ones and Zeros

If your enemy is secure at all points, be prepared for him. If he is in superior strength, evade him. . . . Attack him where he is unprepared, appear where you are not expected.

—Sun Tzu, *The Art of War*

The physician rules the roost in the healthcare world, and there are good reasons for this. The most critical elements in the patient care process could not happen without the providers. This is a given, and the healthcare IT pros would do well to bear this in mind when supporting their most important users.

Dancing through the Dynamics

There is something interesting that happens in many exchanges between physician end-users and the EMR security team or perhaps the chief information security officer, which is not easily explained in the natural "pecking order." Sure, the physicians are the customer of the healthcare IT staff, but in many cases they are the unwilling customer, forced to adopt tools and processes that, in their eyes, get in the way of patient care. Add security measures to clinical workflows, and watch out!

Take a look at how the patient care process has changed in the past decade, and consider the perspective of the physician. At one point, the patient and doctor interacted in an exam room, and the doctor practiced medicine in a very cerebral way, arriving at brilliant conclusions and providing expert care sometimes without even lifting a pen.

The physician's hands, stethoscope, and brain were the primary tools in the provision of care, and perhaps at the end of a patient encounter, some notes and orders were scribbled down. However, it was also just as likely that the doctor's assistant or a nurse would document the encounter and write the orders dictated by the doctor and then pass these along to the doctor for a signature.

Fast-forward to the present day. We have placed a keyboard and a monitor (or a tablet or another digital device) between physicians and their patients, and we require them to document the care they provide and the orders they write into a system that many of them would prefer not to use.

We are still in a phase of adoption where, in the minds of many healthcare providers, the culprit who has placed this obstacle between the physician and his patients is the healthcare IT professional. (It doesn't matter if they intellectually understand that the time for paper has passed and that legislation requiring the use of digital records has pushed the implementation of these apparent obstacles.)

Who can blame a physician for harboring a little resentment toward the EMR implementers? It certainly doesn't help matters much when an analyst comes into a physician's life and presents the new way of doing business through the EMR in inflexible terms. (Certainly none of our own analysts have been guilty of this!)

"I know you used to do things that way, but your new workflow will be _____ ," the novice analyst says—though perhaps only once!

Note　There is a larger discussion about the need for providers to conform to organizational standards of care, including the adoption of standard order sets, workflows, and so on, for the sake of efficiency and improving patient care, but this is not the place for this discussion. The point to be taken here is that EMR implementers should understand the nuanced positions (I pointedly avoid the word *politics* here) that are required to achieve a properly installed EMR.

The bottom line is that many an EMR implementation has taken place without the requisite respect for established norms—and perhaps without adequate acknowledgment that the use of these new tools is indeed going to require work from the physician that was once completed by ancillary staff.

The expectation from the physician is often (sometimes properly), "If you are going to require me to use this EMR system, you are going to make it as painless as possible."

Perhaps some physicians are accustomed to having their requests for efficient workflows go ignored; sometimes their requests are simply not realistic at all.

The bottom line is that when the EMR security guru enters the picture and starts asking questions about the physical environment and the security of the space where the EMR will be used, the natural reaction is quite often, "You're not going to make my workflows more cumbersome are you?"

Reality Recon

Planning for an EMR implementation is often simple until you take your planned workflows out into the trenches where the real work happens each day.

What you soon find is that workflows that seemed just fine will suddenly seem like a bad idea when you walk through it with the providers in the space where care is actually provided.

Consider, for instance, the emergency department.

The emergency department experiences high traffic as multiple care providers enter and leave rooms (or bays) rapidly. You might have a nurse come into a room, document symptoms and check some vitals, then leave (checking back in periodically until a physician is able to tend to the patient).

Now, imagine you are the patient, waiting for 15 minutes, 30 minutes, and then an hour and longer with no sign of a physician. The nurse might come in to check on you every 15 minutes, but as the waiting game progresses, you become curious about what the nurse is documenting in your chart (or if there might be some information about when, or if, you will eventually see a doctor).

The patient, or the patient's family, will be tempted to peek at the chart if proper controls are not in place. Furthermore, the patient will be able to browse his chart and the charts of other patients. The list of other patients waiting to be seen in the department will be good leisure reading to the patient or his family if you don't use caution in how you implement your EMR security.

Simple Solutions

The reality of this scenario dictates some modified workflows that will help mitigate risk in this situation. The clinicians should certainly be asked to lock, secure, or log out of the EMR whenever they leave the patient exam room.

Additionally, high-traffic areas must be protected with additional controls, such as a shorter workstation timeout period, requiring the end-user to unlock the station before continuing to provide care in the EMR.

These simple solutions will often be greeted with a reaction that is understandable but unwarranted, and this is where the security analyst needs to separate the wheat from the chaff.

You might hear something along these lines: "I'm not going to secure my session if I walk out of the room for five minutes. This is simply too inconvenient! I'll be right back, and I'm not going to waste my time with extra keystrokes." (Note that phrase "extra keystrokes"—it will arise repeatedly in your quest to build a lean, efficient EMR.) In cases like these, you need to stop, evaluate the concern as voiced, and consider the validity of the complaint against the risk of exposing patient data.

Note When tasked with finding "physician champions" for your EMR project, it is helpful to gather a broad cross-section of physicians who will enthusiastically support the efforts to digitize patient data. Some senior physicians thrive on new technologies and will be very enthusiastic about EMR adoption. The "new breed" of physician who was raised in the Internet age will expect nothing less than providing care with technology and leveraging the digital tools at his or her disposal to enhance patient care.

Ask yourself this question: "If this end-user were faced with the possibility of leaving his personal online banking session or tax returns up on a computer screen in a room with this stranger, would he feel the same way?" If the answer is no then you need to find a way to push forward with implementing security measures that will protect the vast amount of patient data that sits unprotected every time you leave a workstation unsecured.

You could propose client-based settings that would lock the workstation after several minutes of inactivity, which will probably prompt more than a few people to say, "This is ridiculous. When I walk away from my patient for just a minute and come back to a locked workstation, I am losing precious time."

The reality of the situation is that these are seconds that everyone in an organization must be willing to spend to ensure the confidentiality of patient data. This is where the security analyst needs to be kind, but inflexible.

Think back to the checkered history between the healthcare IT pro and the provider, take a deep breath, and realize that there are some battles where you will need to take a stand and maybe end up with a black eye.

You might start by explaining that your aim of working with all of the providers to ensure efficient workflow is constrained by the obligation we all have to put the patient first by securing patient data in a high-traffic area.

Olive Branches

Your emergency department physician might not be very happy with your decision to put controls in place that require a few extra keystrokes before each encounter. Let's look at other areas where compromise might be possible.

After speaking with the emergency department physician, you discover that he spends most of his time, when he is not in a patient room, at his desk down the hall, researching cases, speaking on the phone, documenting in charts, and placing orders for care.

The key phrase here is "down the hall." On speaking with him a little more, you find out that the area where he sits is designated for him and his colleagues alone.

You ask him, "Would it help you and your colleagues if these workstations didn't go into locked mode until they were inactive for 30 minutes, instead of 10 minutes, which is our standard for most workstations in areas where clinical care is provided?"

This is a small gesture, but this simple accommodation will show your end-users (your customers) that your concern about the safety of patient data extends both ways. When your standards are too lax for some situations, you must modify those. But when your standards can be loosened due to an area's relative physical security, then you can make allowances so that workflows are as efficient as possible.

This will look different in each organization. It is your job to thoroughly evaluate each situation and document your findings and decisions in each case.

Extending some good will in the area of security is perfectly reasonable as long as you are not sacrificing the integrity of patient data. In this scenario, loosening restrictions on workstations in an area where a physician's work is physically isolated from nonemployee traffic and prying eyes will show these physicians that your insistence on best practices where patient data is at the highest risk of exposure is not random, but thoughtful and deliberate.

The Human Element

Although it is certainly noble to implement technologies that will assist in the process of securing patient data, there must always be procedural security measures that are part of workflows in each department.

It shouldn't matter that a session might go into a locked or secure mode after several minutes; end-users should be instructed to always secure their sessions when leaving a workstation unattended.

The location of the workstation is always key here. In a nurse manager's office, where this employee is the only one using the machine day after day, the requirements to secure a machine might not be as stringent.

Imagine the trouble you can encounter when a nurse documents in a patient's chart, leaves the room without securing or logging out of the session, and another care provider comes into the room and begins to document in the chart. Whose name will be associated with the latter notes or documentation? The first nurse, no doubt! What happens when the second care provider enters errant information that leads to a life-threatening health episode? Your compliance office is going to look at who entered the information and prompted the lawsuit (or put the hospital in the position of being susceptible to being sued).

Without a strong element of training in security workflows, technical measures that you put in place will be only partially effective.

Every Workstation Is an Island

Using the Emergency Department as a case study is helpful in determining an approach to the physical and environmental security of the EMR. This lengthy treatment of a single scenario (that might or might not be applicable in your organization) is not supposed to be illustrative of how to approach other scenarios—in other words, it should be a framework that helps you think about this concept.

The following factors that should always be considered in the deployment of a secure EMR:

- **Proximity badges/pass codes:** Is the EMR protected from foot traffic, and prying eyes, by proximity badges or pass codes on doors? Think about the scenario in which a patient is only wheeled into a procedure room after being anesthetized, and family members are never present with the patient. A little more leniency in your security measures can be applied here.

- **Public/reception areas:** Most public waiting or reception areas are staffed by personnel and are rarely left unattended (but there are exceptions). Consider training the front desk employees to keep prying eyes away from their screens, and think about placing covers on monitors that will prevent anyone from seeing content on the screen unless they are directly in front of it.

- **Critical/traumatic care areas:** Standards of screen timeouts, locked screen, and password requirements might be problematic in some areas such as operating rooms, trauma rooms, or surgical pre-op areas where there is a flurry of critical activity and not much time for dealing with extra keystrokes. Consider how you will have to treat these areas in applying security policies.

Common Sense

Your job will not be to adhere to rigid standards, but to interpret the requirements to safeguard patient data in each unique situation. Use your head, and consider what the providers are going through in each scenario, but also consider what the patient would expect of you as the custodian of sensitive data.

There is no magic formula when it comes to applying security standards. This is why the regulations are deliberately vague. The expectation of due diligence, however, is not so vague. It will be abundantly clear if you have been overly accommodating to your user base when it comes to usability.

Always use your best judgment, and never lose sight of the tremendous amount of trust that has been placed in you by your patient population.

Systemwide and Client-Based Security

Making Sure All of the Pieces Fit Together

Leave no stone unturned.

—Euripides, *Heraclidae*

Can you account for all of the devices in your organization? If you are a small facility, or if you have taken on the unenviable task of asset management and succeeded in putting a complex process in place for tracking and keeping up with each of your pieces of equipment, then good for you! This next section will probably be a piece of cake for you.

But if you are like the hosts of organizations that struggle to keep track of exactly where each piece of equipment is at any given time, you will need to pay close attention to this chapter and make a huge point of addressing the complex issue of asset management.

> ▓ **Note** This discussion is not application-specific: the same principles apply regardless of what EMR you chose to implement. Take note of the issues here, and consider how you have or have not considered this aspect of EMR security in your security program.

Imagine a conversation that goes something like this.

"Joe, do we still have two computers in CT Scan Room 9?"

"No, Mark, we stopped using Room 9 about a year ago. I repurposed those computers, and they are now at the main reception area where our volunteers work."

It doesn't take long for a sinking feeling to settle in your stomach. You remember configuring those workstations in CT Scan Room 9 with settings that prevented them from accepting the systemwide security settings that put the EMR into a secured state after 15 minutes. The radiologists were insistent that they needed the extended timeout settings to work efficiently, and your compliance officer and security officer approved that change.

No one informed you that these machines were no longer being used by the radiologists, and certainly no one let you know that the machines were sitting in a public area, being used by the volunteer staff. You knew that they walk away from the machines for coffee breaks on a regular basis.

You go over to the hospital where the volunteers work and make your way to the reception area. As you approach the workstations, you notice that the volunteers have indeed stepped away, and your worst fears are confirmed. Your EMR sits unlocked, open for anyone to browse at their leisure—assuming they are bold enough to pull up a chair and take a stab at learning how to use your system.

If you have implemented your EMR properly, your roles-based access would have limited the volunteers to a very tightly controlled view into the EMR, which is most likely patient names and room numbers (what more do they need?). Still, leaving this information unsecured is not a good plan, and you need to figure out how to manage this situation now and in the future.

A Hierarchy of Settings

What is important to note in the foregoing scenario is that when settings are configurable at the workstation level, this implies that there is a hierarchy, or precedence, in the way that security settings are applied for the users. This flexibility is necessary for areas such as the CT scan room, and it is important that you are able to apply these settings based on the organization's needs. But it is all the more important that you understand the implications of choosing to configure these settings to allow this flexibility.

Here, the workstation security settings obviously supersede the systemwide settings, and what this means for you is that an asset tracking system has to be part of your security management program.

When a device (workstation, tablet, and so on) moves throughout your system, it has to pass through a series of checks to prevent things from running amok quickly—something that is much more costly to clean up than it is to prevent before it becomes a mess in the first place.

It could be that you choose to prevent client-based security settings from being applied in any case because you don't have the staff or processes in place to keep up with the device management process. This is fine, but then you will need to audit the device configuration to ensure that nobody has changed those device-based security settings. If this is your method of security management, then document it, set some calendar reminders to check behind your staff and then document what you find in your audit.

Finally, don't assume you are all set because you have set a universal systemwide security settings for your EMR, and you have a well-managed client-based security process in place.

Some EMR vendors allow access designed for certain roles or positions in an organization to have their own security settings and timeouts. All your surgeons, for instance, could be configured so that they don't have to abide by the systemwide timeout settings regardless of where they login.

Know where these settings are applied and how they might be configured in your EMR. If you have done all of your due diligence in applying and monitoring security settings in other areas of your EMR, but have neglected to keep track of how role-based security settings might have been applied, then you have opened up potentially huge security holes in your EMR.

If you have a surgeon who is configured with these role-based security settings, and he logs into a workstation in a patient room and does not log out, you could be setting yourself up to allow another doctor to come in behind him and start using the system as the surgeon, not realizing the surgeon has not logged out.

All your security settings need to be considered holistically and audited, so that you don't encounter situations that could have been avoided with proper planning and foresight.

Know Your EMR

When all is said and done, the task of understanding and documenting your EMR security settings, and how all of these fit together, must be completed in a manner that your stakeholders can review and understand so that informed decisions can be made about how your organizational policies related to security will be applied.

Most executives and directors don't want a technical white paper or a link to vendor documentation when it comes to the "how" of EMR security. It is the job of the EMR security specialist to break these technical documents down into language that can be digested at all levels of management.

When this task is complete and all your stakeholders have had a chance to weigh in on how your EMR should behave in regard to security, the task of configuring the many settings in your EMR will be much easier.

Most of the discussion in this chapter so far has revolved around timeout settings, and these are important, but it is also important to look at other aspects of security that are configurable within your EMR. The following settings are typically important to the security of your EMR and are configurable at some level within most EMR systems.

- **Timeout behavior:** This is typically the behavior that is expected of your EMR in a number of given situations; this is often configurable to lock the session, log out the user, or close the application after a given time period (configurable in minutes). When a session is locked, you will need to consider how the EMR will behave when another user approaches a locked session; when a session is closed or the application quits, you need to consider what happens to data in sessions that might not have been saved.

- **Directory services integration:** Many EMR systems allow for integration with some flavor of LDAP directory services, and when this is configured many of the security settings can be driven by the network directory services architecture.

- **Password length and complexity:** If you are not pulling password settings from your enterprise LDAP server, then your EMR system will need to drive the password length and complexity settings.

- **Password age:** Again, if you are not pulling these settings from your LDAP server, your EMR system will require users to change their passwords at a given interval, and this is configurable in your EMR system.

- **Et cetera:** Don't assume that because it wasn't mentioned in this list that it isn't pertinent to your security configuration. Comb through the system settings in your EMR and ensure that you understand the effect that they have on the security of your EMR and the confidentiality of your patient data. Without a firm grasp on how your system functions, you can never be sure that you have adequately protected the data you have been charged with protecting.

Know Your Network

You feel like you have done your homework, combing through all of the settings that affect EMR timeout settings, password ages, and more, and you are ready to sit back and focus on more important tasks, right? Well, the reality of the situation is that most devices on a network will have additional settings that govern how they behave on the network, and these have to be considered as you plan your EMR security.

Whether you are using a Microsoft Directory Services Architecture or a Novell eDirectory Network, you will likely have a master "brain" behind the scenes telling your computers and devices when their screensavers should kick in, how many minutes they can be on the network inactive before a password is required, and so on.

If you don't work with your network operations team to ensure that your EMR security settings are configured to work in concert with the enterprise security settings applied to the clients on your network, you will end up with all sorts of situations where workstations are locked but EMR sessions remain active, running in the background.

This task becomes more complex when you begin to configure unique timeout settings in different functional areas, such as surgery or the emergency department. If your EMR security analysts and your network operations folks are on the same page, you will have happy end-users, but if they don't work in concert, you can have some unhappy campers in the end.

Remember, your job is to ensure the security of the EMR and the patient data behind it, but poorly orchestrated security settings that lead to a frustrating user experience will result in your end-users resenting the EMR, and all fingers will end up pointing back at the security team.

Have a game plan, make sure that everything works as planned, and your end-users will be happy with the system you put in place.

Leave No Stone Unturned

Finally, when you are planning out your EMR security, work with each member of your enterprise IT group to understand what might affect your EMR and its operation on your network.

Some EMR deployments introduce new devices that were never part of IT operations before the EMR showed up. If your network engineers have tight controls on the network that require the registration of each new device before it can function, then you will need to take that into account in your security plan.

In the end, you will want to ensure that all aspects of security from end to end have been considered in your plan and documented so that that the end-user has a positive experience and your system remains secure.

Safeguarding Patient Data from Prying Eyes

Knowing Where Your PHI Resides

If you count all your assets, you always show a profit.

—Robert Quillen

The American author and humorist Robert Quillen once joked that anyone could show a profit if he counted all of his assets. In other words, the picture is not always as bleak when you can look at the big picture.

I argue that there is a counterpart to that sense of peace that can come from a broad inventory, and this is a sense of unease that exists when you can't account for things you know you should be able to locate.

"I know I have those tickets to the ball game next week around here somewhere, but I can't remember where I put them!"

Whatever it might be, when we can't account for things that we should be able to locate, our stress levels are elevated, and rightfully so.

Counting Your PHI

Consider the patient data that you have been entrusted with by your customers, the patients under the care of the providers in your organization. If someone were to ask you to give an accounting of where that patient data resides, would you be able to do so?

■ **Note**   Be deliberate in your review of where patient data resides. If you answer, "We have 170 laptops, and I can account for each of these"—be careful. A May 2014 case was settled between the Office of Civil Rights (OCR) and a major New York health system for a data breach that never left the building. A server that contained PHI (think data in a database) was deprovisioned and then repurposed by IT staff. Imagine the joy on the engineer's face when he powered up the server and saw an instance of the database he was going to use already installed and running! The error was discovered when someone was searching for the name of a deceased loved one and found his patient data instead—medications, diagnoses, the works. Almost $5 million in fines later, the health system is addressing this issue holistically in their organization.

If you could not give an accounting of the whereabouts of all of the patient data that might exist in your enterprise, would you be able to give an accounting of the processes and safeguards in place to ensure that it does not go walking outside of your organization or fall into the hands of those who have not signed appropriate confidentiality agreements?

Although providing an accounting of the whereabouts of all the PHI in your organization is not a realistic goal, what you should be able to do as a member of the EMR security team is provide a thorough reckoning of the measures in place to control and regulate the flow of private information in and out of your organization.

Those who fall into the "I-don't-know-what-controls-are-in-place-to-control-our-PHI" camp should certainly be feeling the stress. A little lost sleep is probably in order until you can explain, with confidence, how your organization keeps tabs on its most important digital asset.

■ **Note**   Federal regulations requiring covered entities to disclose breaches of patient data to the government and media outlets are intended to be a negative incentive to put appropriate safeguards in place. The growing "wall of shame" of organizations that have let this sensitive data out of their control proves that some organizations learn their lessons the hard way.

The Anatomy of a Digital Record

Think about a patient chart from days of yore—the manila folder that was chockfull of whatever information the physician deemed important. There could be notes about an episode of pneumonia, a hospital stay for a hip replacement, prescriptions to help control a host of ailments, and interspersed in there myriad orders. There were orders for X-rays during the pneumonia, an MRI from the hip replacement, and so on.

The chart contained notes from the doctor, notes from the nurse, orders placed, and enough information that the provider could pull additional data such as X-ray and MRI images, if necessary.

The new, digitized patient chart contains all of this information, linked together in a meaningful way by the patient identifier or medical record number (MRN). When the patient chart moves from paper to the digital realm, things that might have once existed side by side, such as blood pressure readings and the patient's narrative of symptoms, are suddenly shifted into database tables where they are stored with other types of similar data.

Data segmented like this becomes useful to different segments of your user base for different reasons.

Admission and discharge dates might be useful to your bed planning staff or to those looking at billing reimbursement issues. Mortality and infection statistics can be useful for those looking to improve patient outcomes.

The benefits of a digitized patient chart are innumerable, and you need to make the data available to the people who can use it to improve business processes and patient care. How it gets into their hands is up to the IT staff and organizational leadership.

You should have already ensured that only the right people have access to patient data within your application (recall Chapter 8). Once you've designed your application so that PHI renders properly to your user base, you have to consider how to deliver that data in a more targeted manner to those users.

How to Deliver? Let Me Count the Ways!

The end-user wants data that will assist in the execution of a task or the completion of a job. It isn't much more complicated than that.

There are some critical questions that must be answered about the data you are providing in reports to the end-users—especially when it contains PHI. Consider the following questions, and take them into account when configuring your EMR. These will all need to be factors in your decisions about how data is rendered to the end-user.

- **Will you provide the data in a simple report?** Sometimes users will be content to receive the information they require in a report that renders within the EMR, and that will be the end of the request. This is the simplest and most secure type of request to fulfill.

- **Will the end-user be able to print the report?** As soon as you permit a user to print the report, the PHI in it can easily be scanned and sent around the world with the click of a button (really). When a feature like this is enabled, you must have additional controls in place to regulate the flow of information.

- **Will the end-user be able to save the report?** Similar to the concerns about printing, when the results of a report can be saved to a local hard drive, you have opened yourself up to liabilities that are difficult to control. If a user deletes a file from a hard drive, does it still reside in the "recycle bin" or "trash" on the computer?

- **Can the report results be saved to another format?** Perhaps the users want you to enable saving of the data from the EMR to standard data formats, such as text, CSV, or tab-delimited formats. "This will make it so much easier for me to work with the data," they say. As soon as you allow this, you once again lose control of the data, which can be e-mailed, and, worse, you lose control over the integrity of the results.

That Darned Printer

The questions considered in the preceding section dealt primarily with how your end-users interact with reporting data, but there is also the issue of the ability to print from within your EMR.

Settings in the EMR often allow you to control whether an end-user will be permitted to print various portions of the medical record. The rule of thumb on this privilege is thumbs down. It is after all a digital medical record, and you are trying to consign the paper chart to history!

Be sure you understand how all of these various printing settings work, and don't be caught off guard by the zealous user who will do everything in their power to print that digital chart, even if it means resorting to the "Print Screen" command. Again, a printout can turn into a PDF file and zip across the Internet at lightning speed, and you need to understand all of the moving parts to control them properly.

Finally, how often have you printed something in the office only to arrive at the printer and realize that your printout went somewhere else entirely? "Oh, well," you sigh. "That must have printed at one of the ten other printers I'm connected to. I hope someone will find it and throw it out." This blasé attitude is fine if you are printing the memo about your company picnic. But when PHI involved, the misdirection is much more serious.

The Bigger Picture

If only controlling the flow of data were as simple as a few settings in the EMR. Your job will be to work with the client-server team to ensure that all your bases are covered.

Do you have your EMR deployed through a terminal server such as Citrix that controls how end-users are able to save data? You will need to factor your terminal services configuration into the equation.

In the end, you need to consider all of the client requests for data. (They really do need it—that is the reason the organization spent all of that money on such a fancy system, after all.) And you need to figure out how to provide them what they need in a secure manner.

If you permit any PHI to be saved to workstations in the form of raw data or reports, you will have to ensure that your policy for use of this data is clearly communicated to everyone on staff. Further, you will have to make sure that other teams that might be able to help control the flow of information out of your network (think email, FTP, Internet filesharing sites, and so on) are in the loop and empowered to help you regulate this data, encrypting it if it ever does need to leave your network.

The Inside Job

You know what a danger the end-user can be, and you have developed a plan to control how confidential data flows through your network. All of the proper controls have been put in place within the EMR, and your network operations team is on guard to watch for rogue users who might be circumventing the controls you have put in place.

Your analysts are hard at work ensuring that the EMR is a well-oiled machine, and you have nothing to worry about when it comes to the use or transfer of PHI on their machines, right?

It would be wonderful if the answer to this question were always a resounding yes! The reality is that your own well-meaning folks are often the worst offenders when it comes to handling sensitive data, and a little education goes a long way.

When administrative tools allow for lightning-fast downloading of tables that contain lots of things that you would certainly not want sitting on computers in your organization for any length of time, how do make sure that it doesn't?

Consultants come and go, and computers shuffle around. The best way to handle your administrative staff (and their "elevated access" to patient data) is to set down clear guidelines in policies and enforce violations with penalties when they occur.

The World of Nonprod

Most organizations need for one or more nonproduction environments where support and application build can take place, and these nonproduction environments might contain PHI. Because nonproduction environments tend to be audited less frequently than production EMR environments, organizations need to invest the energy and time to de-identify the patient information to lower its sensitivity in the event of exposure.

■ **Note**   The topic of de-identified data is too large to discuss at any length in this book, but HHS offers some good guidance on this topic on their website and El Emam and Arbuckle treat the topic comprehensively in *Anonymizing Health Data*.

There should also be tight controls over who has access to nonproduction environments, and the IT office should monitor and harden them for any sensitive system. Reality dictates that system administrators, programmers, and other technical staff have access to sensitive information as part of their jobs. The job of IT management is to ensure that their employees are properly controlled and regulated so that the customers (the patients) are confident in the privacy of their data, and the IT staff are enabled to do their jobs.

The standard of minimum necessary should apply here as well, and IT staff such as help desk analysts and ancillary support staff should not be granted full access to the EMR and the patient chart. This access is simply too broad. If your help desk or support staff begin to ask for access to your nonproduction environments for support reasons, you need to evaluate your technologies that permit remote viewing and control of client PCs by these staff members. Why would they need to see the nonproduction environment, when they can see exactly what is on the end-user's screen?

Your production environment is, ideally, the one with real patient data in it. If this is not the case, then build out the storage capacity to audit the environments where you have deemed "real patient data" necessary and put a program in place to audit those environments.

You can make all sorts of claims about the integrity of your system, but if you have a host of mirrored mini-systems that don't undergo the same rigors of your primary system but contain the same data, your claims are rather empty.

Herding Cats . . . or Not

The task of keeping track of the PHI in your EMR system is commonly likened to the Sisyphean labor of "cat herding." But herding cats only becomes a task that you have to undertake if you let them out of the gate in the first place. If you set proper controls in place and keep tabs on where your data is going from the outset, you have a manageable task in front of you.

Most of the requests by end users to be able to print, save data to a local disk, email data, and so on simply are not necessary. A little conversation and some support from your leadership team will go a long way in helping you to keep a tight rein on your data controls. However, once you let the cats out of the bag, the game is over, and I wish you well.

From Project
to Program:
Transitioning
to a Sustainable
Support Model

People, the Most Crucial Element

Training the Masses to Respect the System

What is absurd and monstrous about war is that is that men who have no personal quarrel should be trained to murder one another in cold blood.

—Aldous Huxley, *Words and Behavior*

I happened to be visiting an out-of-town medical system as a patient (not an employee), and I wasn't there even five minutes before I noticed something interesting. The employees in the acute care area, where I was being seen, were extremely diligent about securing their EMR sessions when they stepped more than eight feet from their workstations. This was true for everyone, from the front desk clerk to the clinicians in the back. Like clockwork, they all treated the EMR with the same care, being careful never to leave the system unattended even for a minute or two.

I then noticed something that shed some light on the situation. There were color printouts posted conspicuously around the facility for all to see as a reminder: "Patient Privacy Comes First!" they read. There was some additional verbiage about their privacy incentive and the EMR, but the message was clear. This organization had a policy, and everyone knew what it was.

I don't know if this initiative was the result of a hefty fine for noncompliance, or if there was simply a culture of excellence here (I suspect it was the latter since everything else I experienced in this facility was top notch). One thing was certain—these employees had been trained to behave in a certain way that complied with an organizational policy. This sort of behavior most certainly would not have come about without a clear message and some diligent work on the part of leadership within the organization.

All Together Now: Top–Down!

The discussion of top–down support for security initiatives has been addressed already, and it must be emphasized again in this section on training and human resources.

Without a strong emphasis from leadership on privacy and security, your efforts to secure the EMR will be weak at best. It is imperative that you enlist the support of the highest ranks of leadership in your organization, and that the staff in your organization knows about their support of the security initiatives.

If you try to enforce security as a lone ranger on a quest to protect patient data in your care, you had better find a different battle to fight (or a different job altogether). It simply won't work.

A unified and clear message can have a powerful effect—as illustrated by my story about the organization with festooned with posters proclaiming "Patient Privacy Comes First!"

The first order of business, then, is to ensure that you have the support of your executive leadership team. Then you need to be sure that you partner with the right departments to evangelize your user base with the message you have to share.

Who's Your Partner?

The first order of business is really a negative: "Don't reinvent the wheel."

You are worried about the security of your EMR, and you shouldn't be worried about transforming yourself into an educational guru of sorts. There are people in your organization (one hopes) who are already expert at training others appropriately.

- **Human resources:** The first point of contact with new employees in your organization. Leverage their onboarding process to ensure that privacy and security policies are covered in initial training.

- **Corporate compliance:** Many organizations make their employees undergo some sort of annual compliance training, and there is no reason this should not contain elements of your privacy and security policies and standards. Loop them into your program, and partner with them to get your message across.

- **Information security office:** Your CISO might well have a program established to communicate security standards and policies to the organization. Work with your information security office to ensure that your EMR-specific concerns are addressed in their program.

The end result needs to be a clear message, and your job is to funnel that message through existing channels to make sure that proper practices are followed. The posters on every corner might seem like overkill, but it certainly accomplished its purpose in one organization. Get creative and come up with ways to let your user base know that patient privacy is important to the organization, and everyone has a part to play in helping to make your EMR secure.

Where to Start

The complexities of EMR security would be lost on average users, and there is no need to burden them with details about systemwide security settings and the like. However, the following themes will resonate with all your users.

- **Password privacy:** It might seem like common sense, but users need to be reminded that their passwords cannot reside on a yellow sticky note on their monitor.

- **Password sharing:** Another obvious one for most users, sharing a password (especially a provider sharing a password so that an assistant can login and complete work in their name) should never be allowed. Password sharing for the purposes of support by IT staff should also never be permitted—there are other ways to accomplish your goals. Any violations of this rule should be dealt with swiftly and formally when brought to the attention of leadership.

- **Removable media:** Though technical standards should prohibit the transfer of private information to removable media in most cases, your end-users should absolutely certain that no PHI should leave the organization on removable media such as thumb drives.

- **E-mail:** What is acceptable to e-mail and what is not? Contrary to popular opinion, that paragraph of pseudo-legalese appended to the end of many e-mails is really not a legal safeguard. A real safeguard is a properly educated user base and an email system with some intelligence that can look for PHI. Never send unencrypted PHI via email, ever.

- **Mobile devices and patient data:** More organizations are adopting a BYOD (bring your own device) policy with their employees, and the healthcare space is no exception. If you are going to allow end-users to use their own devices such as smartphones or iPads, then you have to communicate acceptable parameters of use.

The list of things that you could address with your end-users goes on and on. The important thing is that your user base becomes acquainted with your standards of privacy and security in the same way they are familiar with standards of ethics and conduct. They would not dream of stealing from their organization—this would manifestly be unacceptable. In the same way, they should never dream of compromising the integrity of the patient data they have access to by virtue of their job.

Hearts and Minds

It might seem like overkill to liken the fight to promote a culture of privacy and security to a battle for the hearts and minds of your users, but when all is said and done, this is really what it is all about.

If you don't convince your employees that this is a worthy endeavor, that there really is a sacred trust given to each of them when they open up the patient chart and access data that is some of the most private information people have to share, then the battle is lost.

Your employees will search for their neighbor's chart because they can. They will speak callously about a sensitive diagnosis with their coworkers because they find it humorous. They will transmit and store all sorts of private information without giving a second thought to what they are risking if that data is lost.

You have to first build a system that discourages the misuse of patient data, and then teach your employees that what they do have access to is terribly important and must not be misused.

Business Associates

The Human Resources Just Beyond Your Reach

Доверяй, но проверяй. (Doveryai, no proveryai—Trust, but verify.)

—Russian proverb

It was the eleventh hour of an EMR implementation project, and pressure was mounting. The existing system was finely tuned, and community physicians throughout the region had access to their patients' records when they were admitted to the hospital. The same was expected with the new EMR.

"Where are my credentials for the new system?" was the common refrain echoed by physicians throughout the region. We learned to reply, "Did you return your business associate agreement? Let me put you in touch with the person coordinating that process."

Physician access to patient data—X-ray images, pathology results, and so on—is essential to providing an appropriate continuum of care. Moreover, any healthcare organization must provide its community physicians with access to this essential data if they they continue to refer patients to them for procedures. This is how healthcare organizations stay in business, after all.

There are two conditions under which a covered entity will provide access to its EMR without a *business associate agreement* (BAA):

- If the user is an employee of the entity

- If the user is *credentialed* by the entity to provide care in the entity

Everyone that doesn't fall into one of these two categories is classified as a *business associate* and required to sign a BAA.

Note A sample BAA is provided for your use and adaptation at the end of this book. If you don't have a BAA in place or if it could use some refining, now would be a good time to consider this important aspect of your security program.

What's in a Name?

By definition, a *business associate* is someone with whom you have a business relationship and who has some sort of indirect relationship with your organization. That's where the cut-and-dried nature of a business associate ends.

The reality of the situation is that a business associate could be anyone from a consultant working to implement your EMR to a traveling nurse brought in to augment your nursing staff on a temporary basis. These people don't report directly to you, and they are most often paid by a third party—although that third party could very likely receive the money to pay them from your organization.

As in the example with the community physicians just described, some business associates are not paid as a result of work done on behalf of your organization, but your organization has a vested interest in providing them with access to PHI in your possession. Therefore, they are business associates.

It does not matter why you have provided access to your EMR or patient data—the possible reasons are many and diverse. What matters is that the access is *necessary*. The important fact is that these business associates have been entrusted with something of a sensitive nature, and they must be held accountable for that trust.

Trust, but verify!

What Do You Give Them?

What you provide your business associates should be contextually appropriate under the minimum necessary standard, just as for your employees' access. In particular, the following access equivalences (neither more nor less) apply:

- **Agency nurses** should have the same access as your standard nurses.
- **Consultant IT staff** should have the same access as your **equivalent** in-house IT staff.
- **Contract housekeeping staff** should have the same access as your equivalent in-house housekeeping staff.

Users of these and similar types fall under the business associate umbrella. In the end you must use common sense when granting access to your digital assets to your nonemployee users and make sure that you have signed BAAs on file for every one of them. The cascading nature of BAAs can get a little tricky. You might, for instance, have a signed BAA with an organization that provides services to you, and that organization might, in turn, have BAAs for each of its subcontractors that are working for you on behalf of your business partner. You should secure a signed BAA for each person with a named account in your EMR.

HHS requires that any security violation or privacy breach by a business associate be treated the same as an infraction by an employee. If a business associate misplaces a laptop that is not yours but that contains PHI from your organization, you are obliged to report the violation. There is no difference in the eyes of the law in this regard. This general approach covers those contract workers who are functioning as employees of your organization but otherwise unaccountable to your HR structure.

Note   In addition to a sample BAA, sample rules of behavior and an agreement for privileged use (administrative access) are provided at the end of this book for use in your organization. You may use this, adapted for your organization's needs, as you see fit. It is important that your business associates with privileged-use accounts sign such an agreement and all of your administrative users review and sign such an agreement so that a clear framework for acceptable use is established and agreed on.

What about those physicians who want or need access to your EMR in order to facilitate their own business and patient care workflows but not as part of care in your organization? Outside the realm of equivalent roles, such as credentialed providers, the lines become fuzzy and compliance with the minimum necessary standard requires nuanced judgment on your part.

Community physicians, for example, need access to lab results and X-rays to provide patient care. The access you provide them may take any of several forms, as discussed in the following section.

A Targeted View

The needs of a particular community physician fall into one of two categories:

- The provider requires access to your EMR records of patients who are under his or her care in the practice that he or she works in or manages.

- The provider requires access to your EMR records of patients from their practice who have been recently seen in your facility.

Either way, there should be no necessity for a physician who is neither employed by your organization nor credentialed with your medical staff office to have full access to your master patient index. Whether or not your organization has the technological capabilities or the expertise to segment the patients as outlined above is another matter altogether.

Most EMR vendors sell systems and technologies that allow organizations to funnel patients to community providers based on their need to know. Certainly you must be willing and able to oblige a community physician whose patient was in your hospital for pneumonia and who requests access to the patient's chart for that stay. Healthcare systems want community providers to have access to that kind of information. If it is nearly impossible for a community provider to find out what happened with her patient during an encounter in a hospital, then she will likely refer her patients in future to a hospital that makes the process easier. Who can blame her?

Provide this link to targeted patient data! If you are providing access to a pool of patient data that is too broad, then craft a project plan to address the issue.

Remember, patient privacy is a fiduciary as well as regulatory matter. You owe it to your patients to ensure that you provide access to their records only to authorized entities and strictly on a need-to-know basis.

Other Areas of Risk

"Nothing is quite so black and white!" your executives and directors are apt to say. "This person or that organization has always had access to our charts for one reason or another, and we need to continue to provide this access. It is just good business!"

In cases like this, you need to think at a deeper level. What is really being provided to this person or organization when they have access to your EMR or master patient index?

Poachers

Think about the case of a nursing home or home health agency with whom you have had a great working relationship over the years. These business associates have always been there to answer your phone calls when other business associates weren't.

"We need to provide access to these folks," one of your vice presidents says.

What happens if your favored business associates don't just use the EMR to review the charts of their patients but begin to do preemptive "customer poaching"—looking for prime targets to fill their rosters when business is slow. Perhaps they will look for patients who have been admitted for more than two or three weeks or those with certain diagnoses or conditions. Your EMR has next of kin and emergency contact information listed in the chart. How easy would it be to place a marketing call in advance of what will surely be a difficult discharge for these patients?

This might seem like good business on one level, but ask yourself: Have you thereby provided an unfair advantage to selected business associates?

Furthermore, this kind of use of patient data is ethically questionable. Case managers and social workers in hospitals are prepared to handle discharge planning in an equitable manner—they most certainly don't need business managers poaching their patients before they have been given orders to leave the hospital.

Teleworkers

There is also the matter of the contract employee whom you never see—who was perhaps enlisted to help with a project that is labor-intensive and requires many people working countless hours to accomplish a task. *Abstraction* is a good example of such a task: data from one system needs to be abstracted into another system, most often a new EMR. Companies that specialize in this service and use an entirely remote staff are called on to help get the job done.

What do you get when you enlist the assistance of a remote abstraction service? Perhaps many diligent and faithful workers, but you are also likely to get a handful of people who responded to postings on online job boards promising above minimum wage for a work-at-home job.

You would like to think that these remote abstractors are all isolated in a home offices furnished by the healthcare IT company with dedicated equipment and software closely protected by passwords and screensavers.

What is all too likely, however, is that these computers are in somebody's living room in a suburban home and are used for children's homework and video games when the abstraction work isn't being done. They might or might not have decent antivirus software, and they probably aren't in discreet locations where others can't see what is on the screen.

Are you better off with your head in the sand? I think not.

The best approach is, perhaps, to work with the vendors who provide such services and ask them what sort of employees they use to accomplish this kind of work. Chances are good that you can find a company who holds their workers to higher standards, provides equipment (and even benefits) for them, and ensures privacy and security for their customers' data.

It's Not about Payroll

When you work through the matter of business associates in your organization, you would do well to avoid looking at this as a matter to cross off of your compliance to-do list.

This is not about ensuring that you have a piece of paper signed by each of your nonemployees who happens to have access to sensitive information. (If only it were that simple.)

Again, think about the trust that your customers, the patients, have reposed in your organization, and then consider what sort of access they would expect you to give to people who are not employees of your organization.

Furthermore, what sort of checks and balances are in place to ensure that your business associates are held to the same high standards to which you hold your own employees? What does it matter if your own managers keep excellent tabs on their employees' use of the EMR, but you don't track or control how your business partners use the same data? What good is it if your own equipment is safeguarded from prying eyes and tightly controlled with passwords and antivirus software if you don't have any control over the same when it comes to your business associates?

Having that signed piece of BAA paper is necessary but not sufficient. You must independently satisfy yourself of the integrity and responsibility of your business associates in the way they conduct business with your organization.

Trust, but verify!

Security Project versus Operational Support

Making the Transition

We shall defend our island, whatever the cost may be, we shall fight on the beaches, we shall fight on the landing grounds, we shall fight in the fields and in the streets, we shall fight in the hills; we shall never surrender.

—Winston Churchill, June 4, 1940

My wife often hands me a healthy, and well deserved, dose of ridicule for planning my plans. I often have worked through the details of a family vacation, as I envision how a good vacation might look, months before sharing my thoughts about it with my family. I am known for having a complex web of plans with dependencies and contingencies, all worked out in my head long before I put them down on paper. This is just how I am wired.

Criticisms about my tendency to let these plans get too far along before sharing them with those who need to know humbly acknowledged, it is nonetheless important to recognize the importance of working diligently on the task at hand with frequent glances at the horizon. We need to keep our eyes on what is coming down the road if we are to greet the future with success.

The second habit in Stephen Covey's *The Seven Habits of Highly Effective People* is to "begin with the end in mind." To attain successful outcomes, it is imperative to prefigure and visualize the goals to be realized.

As you work through your project, don't forget to glance up regularly at the next step, which is the transition to operational support.

Weary, but Ready for What's Next

You have worked long hours to understand the complex maze of regulatory requirements. You have assembled a team of top-notch people to ensure that everyone who needs to be at the table is there. You've surveyed your environment so you know what you are dealing with, and you dusted off all of those old policies that hadn't seen the light of day in quite a long time.

With much sweat, and perhaps a few tears, you ensure that you know who your users are, and you develop systems to track them. You design a tight application that permits your users to access what is appropriate to their roles, and you tweak access for all the different scenarios in your organization.

Servers and clients are speaking to each other. System settings are interacting with devices as expected.

Your users are trained, and they know their responsibilities in keeping patient data safe.

When you sit back after the dust of your EMR launch settles, and you survey the system that you put in place, you will perhaps get a feeling of accomplishment and be tempted to put your feet up on the desk, or schedule that long vacation you have been meaning to take.

The vacation might not be a bad idea, but the post-EMR go-live phase is not the time to sit back and listen to the engine purr; it's the time for optimization. This is true with application workflows and business processes, and it is just as true with your security processes. The words at the forefront of your mind should be *security program*.

Whether you have a well-oiled security program in place in your organization or unrefined and undocumented processes, you need to be thinking program. You have implemented a secure EMR (or perhaps, with the help of this book, you retroactively applied the same principles that you would have employed if you had this book in the beginning). The next section addresses the question: Now that your EMR security project is complete, what do you do next?

Reduce, Reuse, Recycle

In the lead-up to a go-live, you typically ramp up the staffing, bringing on temporary help to ensure that you have all of the success you hoped for. Your team, which worked hard to get through the implementation, is proud of the success that was achieved with a great deal of effort.

Your end-users get used to the new system, things that seemed difficult to support become second nature to your staff, and then people start to wonder what shoes they will fill now that the press and the urgency of the big project has subsided.

The temporary staff members will go back to wherever they were before, unless you find that a few are simply too valuable to release. Some of your project team members were functioning in operational roles all along, and those roles will continue after the launch of the new system.

The reality of the situation is that you will lose some of your project staff as a result of natural attrition. They might simply decide that the EMR world is not for them, or perhaps they are ready for something else. A natural reduction in team size is going to happen in every project without a master plan; this is simply how things work.

Other members of your team will probably be repurposed in the post-implementation world. Some of the people who join the EMR project team as analysts find that they really aren't analysts at all, but the knowledge of the EMR that they gained is valuable to the organization. Perhaps these repurposed analysts will best serve the organization in the role of a trainer or clinical IT support staff. Maybe some of your revenue cycle analysts will go to work in the billing office.

Note The value of a clinical informatics or EMR help desk cannot be overstated, and it is probably best to put your long-term support plans for the EMR in place before you launch it. Perhaps you don't know each employee who will staff this help desk well in advance of your go-live but you will certainly want to have a support paradigm mapped out and in hand before you flip the switch.

It is important that your managers look at the project team's human resources carefully to determine where they will best serve the organization and where they will be happiest working. The time to begin planning for this phase of operational transition is before the launch of your EMR. You certainly can't make all of the HR, budgetary, and other decisions before you know the hand you have been dealt. But a little advanced planning will serve your managers and your team members well.

The application analysts who were building your application will likely be needed to support the application, and you will probably find a post-implementation support team that looks a lot like your implementation team. Build on the strengths of your best employees, encourage them to develop their skills, and make sure that you are using everyone to the best of their abilities.

The Groups: What to Do with Them?

Your project team members have found positions in one place or another, but you have functional groups, such as your security workgroup and your security stakeholders, that you convened to accomplish particular purposes. These functional groups have learned to work well together, and they know how to address security issues and work through a process to find a solution. This is something you probably don't want to abandon, but you might not need to meet with the frequency that was required during implementation.

You will need to evaluate your needs in each of these functional areas, and determine how you will use these existing groups to accomplish new goals. Develop a charter for each of these groups so that there is no question about the purpose of their existence. Does the group name need to change? Does the composition of the group need to shuffle a bit? These are all issues that must be addressed as you make the transition from project to operational support.

Note   Groups without a clear purpose or charter will not be well attended, and participation will be lackluster. Be very deliberate about how you use your employees' time, and they will respect that in most cases by returning the favor with quality output.

Your security workgroup might well exist as a standing group to vet proposed changes in security functionality to the EMR. Instead of dealing with the constant addition of new roles and talking through new build issues, these members can be the sounding board of reason before your stakeholders receive the final request for access changes.

The stakeholders can function as they did before—as the gatekeepers of access-related decisions that your users might be tempted to push through as productivity enhancements.

How Is the EMR Being Used?

Once you give access to the users in your organization, you would be negligent if you simply assumed they were abiding by the rules that you have laid out for them. Yes, they should only access the record of patients that are in their immediate care, but there will be employees that will be looking up the records of family members during a slow night shift. Perhaps someone is looking up the records of their spouse, with whom they are struggling through an acrimonious divorce, anxious for some dirt to use in the long, drawn-out fight.

The only way that you will find these abuses of your patient data is if you proactively look for suspect patterns of use, such as users who access patient data with the same last name or patient records in which the street address is the same as their own.

The good news is that there are reasonably priced third-party systems that help in the process of reporting on these misuses of patient data. Post-implementation is the time to start meeting with these vendors. Reach out to them and find out how they can help you work to keep your EMR secure.

Most EMR systems also provide the ability to create reports for compliance reporting purposes, and these can be configured and used free of charge. Take advantage of this ability. Make sure that reports are gathering the data you need and that they are delivered to people who can interpret the results in a meaningful way ... which leads you to the matter of personnel.

Some of your project team members need to be repurposed, and what better way to do so than to give them the important job of working closely with your compliance office to audit the use of your EMR? Reports and reporting tools are useless and worthless if you don't have the right people assigned to receive and interpret the data.

Finally, what do you do when you discover violators of your policies on EMR use? This is an area where many organizations struggle unnecessarily.

The short answer should be: "When employees misuse patient data, we discipline them immediately and, if necessary, terminate their employment."

When your audits show a pattern of misuse by your employees, there has to be a well-documented process that your managers will follow in disciplining the violators. Employees should be quite certain that discovery of their misuse of the system will incur clearly prescribed disciplinary action.

Changes

One thing is certain: You cannot count on things to remain the same in your environment. As soon as you think that you have a handle on things, a regulation will change, requiring you to adapt your practices, or you will upgrade your system and need to change your technical approach to EMR security.

Consider system upgrades, for example. Many of the security processes that you put in place around your EMR are based on how the EMR works for you today. Some of these processes are cumbersome, but they have to be that way because there isn't a better way to do them.

Fast-forward to the next release of your EMR software. You take the upgrade, begin to do the daily work that you did before, and notice that there are new buttons and functions available that affect how you accomplish security-related processes.

You have to be ready to modify your processes when changes come your way. Stop—don't panic. Think through the issues, whatever they might be. Document your new process, communicate it to the appropriate staff members, and move on.

Other changes are going to be introduced as a result of new technologies. The next release of your EMR software might make the use of phones for certain EMR functions a viable option for the first time. This innovation is going to affect your security program, and you will need to document and accommodate accordingly.

What is important in the grand scheme of things is the willingness to be flexible and the ability to adapt. Always look at change through the lens of privacy and security. Not all changes introduced into your environment will have an impact on security, but you would be surprised at the number of changes that do have an effect, large or small. It is your job to take note of these and react accordingly.

Integration

There is a tendency to look at your EMR as an island unto itself, but the reality of the situation is that it is one of your enterprise IT applications, albeit perhaps the core application.

You might be tempted to see the cohesive nature of your EMR team as a good thing and build on that, but it is probably better to look for ways to integrate your EMR team into the IT staff as quickly as possible after the go-live.

There are several ways you can do this: cross-training, colocation of teams, combined workspaces, and frequent and combined meetings. Get creative, and do your best to inculcate the sense in your EMR analysts that they are IT employees and they need to function as such.

If your EMR team members are allowed to do so, they might cloister themselves off and become experts in repetitive tasks that are not very technological at all. If the tasks are repetitive, then document them, share them with others, and have your employees who are inclined toward repetitive tasks learn a new skill in the department.

There are some bad habits that can creep into an EMR team, and myopic insularity is one that doesn't serve the organization well. Remember, the EMR is a giant IT tool, and the people who support it are IT employees who need to function as such.

Note   Chapter 8 stressed the importance of ensuring that your analysts are able to analyze. Making sure you have the right person for the job is very important in the staffing process, and it is likewise important that you integrate your EMR analysts into the IT office to reinforce the nature of the work at hand.

When it comes to your EMR security team specifically, in a similar way you will want to work to ensure that they know their role in the world of your IT security office. Be sure that your IT security staff members are aware of the EMR security processes and tasks that take place on a regular basis.

Get your EMR security team members involved in the broader IT security functions that are happening. Encourage team members to shift roles for a month to cross-train and understand the big picture. Have your help desk or provisioning team members work with the EMR team to understand what goes into the access they are creating. The more your teams are aware of what their colleagues are doing, the more secure your organization will be. Everyone must have a specialty, and you certainly have to allow people to function in their primary role most of the time, but don't be afraid to let people venture outside their comfort zones. When you do this, everyone wins.

Change Control

The change control process in your organization needs representation from your security team. Change control processes are often the bane of many an IT organization's existence. The meetings are boring, and the process of documenting changes seems cumbersome at times.

Think about what happens when your change control board representatives are reviewing changes without a representative from the security team. Changes that might seem perfectly acceptable and viable to the board will be approved if the security representative doesn't chime in with his input, which is filtered through a lens that only he possesses.

Whatever your process was for approving changes before your implementation—and it was probably more fluid before your go-live—be sure that your EMR security is well represented on your change control board, or you will find yourself fighting security fires that didn't need to start in the first place.

Enjoy

- When all is said and done, you will need to ensure that you have made a clear transition from project mode to operations gracefully by mapping out in writing what this looks like. Then, after a time, evaluate your success by reviewing your goals.

- The energy of a big project cannot be matched, but there is a certain measure of joy that comes from looking at the results of your work and taking pride in a job well done. Take pride when you walk into the doctor's office and see the system that you implemented being used to facilitate your care.

- It was no small task.

Putting the Plan in Place

Ongoing Maintenance and Life after the Security Project

Integrity without knowledge is weak and useless, and knowledge without integrity is dangerous and dreadful.

—Samuel Johnson, *The History of Rasselas, Prince of Abissinia*

It is daunting, even frightening, to be thrown into the deep end in any situation, including the world of EMR security. This book is not an encyclopedia of healthcare IT security but a toolbox for anyone—technical, management, or executive—with responsibility for a secure EMR.

Because this book is deliberately vendor-agnostic and does not detail precise solutions for specific products, you might still be perplexed about a unique situation that you are facing.

The purpose of a toolbox is to help you march into a project with a fighting chance at a successful outcome. Every situation is different and, just as in any home improvement project that you might undertake, you might find yourself running out for another tool or looking for additional assistance where your skills fall short.

I remember the feeling I got about a week into a fixer-upper home purchase. My teenage son and I were feeling defeated as we tried to make the home habitable so that the rest of the family could leave our previous home in New York and join us at our new home near the beach in North Carolina.

We were competent and we had plenty of tools, but several things quickly became apparent to us. We certainly didn't have the skills to complete all of the tasks at hand. I discovered that plumbing is very unforgiving, and a hobbyist would do well to leave plumbing repairs to the pros. Some of the tools that we needed to accomplish the job weren't in our toolboxes and were too expensive to purchase.

With some phone calls and networking in our new town, we were able to get the home in shape, and the rest of the family joined us about a month later.

Was our toolbox useless? Were we incompetent? No, not at all. We simply needed to augment our tools with the tools and skills of others. When we shifted gears a bit, we saw some great successes.

We now take great pride in our fixer-upper home, having expended blood, sweat, and tears to get to its current state. I avoid saying "never" in life, but undertaking another fixer-upper home is something I will never do again. I also couldn't be more proud of the project that my son and I almost wrote off as hopeless.

The EMR security project—taken in its totality with all related tasks—can seem like a huge, impossible task, but it is not. It is worthwhile and something that you can take pride in if you use the tools at your disposal and some extra help along the way when necessary.

Don't Forget the Project Plan

It doesn't matter how large or small your organization is, you have to break everything down, prioritize, and then figure out how the work is going to be accomplished.

I worked for a while without formal training in project management, and I realized at one point that I needed a framework to guide me through the many varied tasks that I had on my plate at any given time. This led me to study and sit the Project Management Professional (PMP) exam, and I must say that the tools and knowledge I gained in the process were invaluable. There are other project management certifications out there, and the training options are innumerable. Trying to get complex parallel and interdependent tasks done without a plan and a framework is to set yourself up for failure.

If you don't have the requisite project management skills to put a plan together, then run (don't walk) to the nearest colleague who can assist you in the process. Your organization's project management office (PMO) is the most logical place to start, but many organizations don't have a well-oiled PMO in place. If you are in a small shop and don't have a network of people to use as resources, then attending a local chapter meeting of the Project Management Institute (PMI) would be a good place to start.

Make notes, figure out what needs to be accomplished, prioritize those tasks, and then put a formal plan in place.

When All Is Said and Done

Fast-forward six months, one year, or five years. You have planned and conquered. The issues that once seemed most daunting and unconquerable are resolved and your solutions are in place. Your EMR security efforts have been integrated into the security program, and people know their jobs, their roles, and how to do what it takes to keep your patient data secure.

There is a concept in the world of project management called *rebaselining*, which is employed when enough variables in your project have changed to warrant a reevaluation of your project as a whole. When your project is complete and closed, there is nothing to rebaseline. However, you can certainly pull out your tool chest (including this book and any other tools you might have amassed along the way) and take stock again in the environment that you manage. Perhaps your thinking will have evolved or matured in one domain or another. Maybe an inelegant solution that you implemented as a stop-gap measure can be refined thanks to new funding that is now available.

Your policies will need to be updated on a regular basis as workflows change, and new employees will certainly need to be integrated into the culture of privacy and security that you have worked hard to develop. The core issues of privacy and security that you work through now will need to be reassessed and reevaluated based on the new information that comes into scope.

Nonetheless, once you have addressed something well and put solid processes place, you won't need to spin your wheels going back to the same issue time after time. Take pride the success of a great solution, and shift your focus to areas that could use some improvement. They will always exist.

Don't Forget Why

In the press of a project or with a mandate to "get a handle on security," it is often difficult to keep your focus on the reason why privacy and security are things to worry about in the first place. It isn't on your plate because of looming fines or the threat of legal penalties for lack of compliance. These are incentives, but they are not the fundamental rationale for privacy and security initiatives.

Remember the sensitive nature of the data that you house, the amount of trust that patients place in their providers, and consider the fact that how each patient's personal information is handled is a reflection on how an organization respects its patients.

It isn't any more complicated than that.

A callous or cavalier approach to EMR privacy and security is simply lack of respect for people—neighbors, friends, parents, grandparents, and children, including those of hospital and physician practice employees. The hospital, the physician practice, the insurance company, the third-party employee, and everyone else in the lineup are obliged to do whatever it takes to secure the digitized patient chart not because of laws, new or old, but because it is simply the right thing to do.

When you approach your charge to secure patient data from this ethical starting point, you will ultimately be successful. When you show your superiors that your requests for funds are necessary because it is the right thing to do and because it makes financial sense, you are more likely to get the green light. When you introduce a new, more secure process to your physician users because you care about doing what is right for the patients and because it will help the organization avoid costly fines, they are more likely to fall in line.

Look beyond the legislation that is pushing the project to the reason for the legislation, and you will be on a solid footing.

Appendices

Sample Business Associate Agreement

> **Note** The following *business associate agreement* is boilerplate language provided by the United States Department of Health and Human Services.[1] It is in the public domain and may be used/modified by your organization as you deem appropriate.

Sample Business Associate Agreement Provisions

Introduction

A "business associate" is a person or entity, other than a member of the workforce of a covered entity, who performs functions or activities on behalf of, or provides certain services to, a covered entity that involve access by the business associate to protected health information. A "business associate" also is a

---

[1] U.S. Department of Health and Human Services, "Business Associates Contracts: Sample Business Associate Agreement Provisions," January 25, 2013. http://www.hhs.gov/ocr/privacy/hipaa/understanding/coveredentities/contractprov.html.

subcontractor that creates, receives, maintains, or transmits protected health information on behalf of another business associate. The HIPAA Rules generally require that covered entities and business associates enter into contracts with their business associates to ensure that the business associates will appropriately safeguard protected health information. The business associate contract also serves to clarify and limit, as appropriate, the permissible uses and disclosures of protected health information by the business associate, based on the relationship between the parties and the activities or services being performed by the business associate. A business associate may use or disclose protected health information only as permitted or required by its business associate contract or as required by law. A business associate is directly liable under the HIPAA Rules and subject to civil and, in some cases, criminal penalties for making uses and disclosures of protected health information that are not authorized by its contract or required by law. A business associate also is directly liable and subject to civil penalties for failing to safeguard electronic protected health information in accordance with the HIPAA Security Rule.

A written contract between a covered entity and a business associate must: (1) establish the permitted and required uses and disclosures of protected health information by the business associate; (2) provide that the business associate will not use or further disclose the information other than as permitted or required by the contract or as required by law; (3) require the business associate to implement appropriate safeguards to prevent unauthorized use or disclosure of the information, including implementing requirements of the HIPAA Security Rule with regard to electronic protected health information; (4) require the business associate to report to the covered entity any use or disclosure of the information not provided for by its contract, including incidents that constitute breaches of unsecured protected health information; (5) require the business associate to disclose protected health information as specified in its contract to satisfy a covered entity's obligation with respect to individuals' requests for copies of their protected health information, as well as make available protected health information for amendments (and incorporate any amendments, if required) and accountings; (6) to the extent the business associate is to carry out a covered entity's obligation under the Privacy Rule, require the business associate to comply with the requirements applicable to the obligation; (7) require the business associate to make available to HHS its internal practices, books, and records relating to the use and disclosure of protected health information received from, or created or received by the business associate on behalf of, the covered entity for purposes of HHS determining the covered entity's compliance with the HIPAA Privacy Rule; (8) at termination of the contract, if feasible, require the business associate to return or destroy all protected health information received from, or created or received by the business associate on behalf of, the covered entity; (9) require the business associate to ensure that any subcontractors it may engage on its behalf that will have access to protected health information agree to the same restrictions and conditions that apply to the business associate with respect to such information; and (10) authorize termination of the contract by the covered entity if the business associate violates a material term of the contract. Contracts between business associates and business associates that are subcontractors are subject to these same requirements.

This document includes sample business associate agreement provisions to help covered entities and business associates more easily comply with the business associate contract requirements. While these sample provisions are written for the purposes of the contract between a covered entity and its business associate, the language may be adapted for purposes of the contract between a business associate and subcontractor.

This is only sample language and use of these sample provisions is not required for compliance with the HIPAA Rules. The language may be changed to more accurately reflect business arrangements between a covered entity and business associate or business associate and subcontractor. In addition, these or similar provisions may be incorporated into an agreement for the provision of services between a covered entity and business associate or business associate and subcontractor, or they may be incorporated into a separate business associate agreement. These provisions address only concepts and requirements set forth in the HIPAA Privacy, Security, Breach Notification, and Enforcement Rules, and alone may not be sufficient to result in a binding contract under State law. They do not include many formalities and substantive provisions that may be required or typically included in a valid contract. Reliance on this sample may not be sufficient for compliance with State law, and does not replace consultation with a lawyer or negotiations between the parties to the contract.

Sample Business Associate Agreement Provisions

Words or phrases contained in brackets are intended as either optional language or as instructions to the users of these sample provisions.

Definitions

Catch-all definition

The following terms used in this Agreement shall have the same meaning as those terms in the HIPAA Rules: Breach, Data Aggregation, Designated Record Set, Disclosure, Health Care Operations, Individual, Minimum Necessary, Notice of Privacy Practices, Protected Health Information, Required By Law, Secretary, Security Incident, Subcontractor, Unsecured Protected Health Information, and Use.

Specific definitions

(a) <u>Business Associate</u>. "Business Associate" shall generally have the same meaning as the term "business associate" at 45 CFR 160.103, and in reference to the party to this agreement, shall mean [Insert Name of Business Associate].

(b) <u>Covered Entity</u>. "Covered Entity" shall generally have the same meaning as the term "covered entity" at 45 CFR 160.103, and in reference to the party to this agreement, shall mean [Insert Name of Covered Entity].

(c) <u>HIPAA Rules</u>. "HIPAA Rules" shall mean the Privacy, Security, Breach Notification, and Enforcement Rules at 45 CFR Part 160 and Part 164.

Obligations and Activities of Business Associate

Business Associate agrees to:

(a) Not use or disclose protected health information other than as permitted or required by the Agreement or as required by law;

(b) Use appropriate safeguards, and comply with Subpart C of 45 CFR Part 164 with respect to electronic protected health information, to prevent use or disclosure of protected health information other than as provided for by the Agreement;

(c) Report to covered entity any use or disclosure of protected health information not provided for by the Agreement of which it becomes aware, including breaches of unsecured protected health information as required at 45 CFR 164.410, and any security incident of which it becomes aware;

[The parties may wish to add additional specificity regarding the breach notification obligations of the business associate, such as a stricter timeframe for the business associate to report a potential breach to the covered entity and/or whether the business associate will handle breach notifications to individuals, the HHS Office for Civil Rights (OCR), and potentially the media, on behalf of the covered entity.]

(d) In accordance with 45 CFR 164.502(e)(1)(ii) and 164.308(b)(2), if applicable, ensure that any subcontractors that create, receive, maintain, or transmit protected health information on behalf of the business associate agree to the same restrictions, conditions, and requirements that apply to the business associate with respect to such information;

(e) Make available protected health information in a designated record set to the [Choose either "covered entity" or "individual or the individual's designee"] as necessary to satisfy covered entity's obligations under 45 CFR 164.524;

[The parties may wish to add additional specificity regarding how the business associate will respond to a request for access that the business associate receives directly from the individual (such as whether and in what time and manner a business associate is to provide the requested access or whether the business associate will forward the individual's request to the covered entity to fulfill) and the timeframe for the business associate to provide the information to the covered entity.]

(f) Make any amendment(s) to protected health information in a designated record set as directed or agreed to by the covered entity pursuant to 45 CFR 164.526, or take other measures as necessary to satisfy covered entity's obligations under 45 CFR 164.526;

[The parties may wish to add additional specificity regarding how the business associate will respond to a request for amendment that the business associate receives directly from the individual (such as whether and in what time and manner a business associate is to act on the request for amendment or whether the business associate will forward the individual's request to the covered entity) and the timeframe for the business associate to incorporate any amendments to the information in the designated record set.]

(g) Maintain and make available the information required to provide an accounting of disclosures to the [Choose either "covered entity" or "individual"] as necessary to satisfy covered entity's obligations under 45 CFR 164.528;

[The parties may wish to add additional specificity regarding how the business associate will respond to a request for an accounting of disclosures that the business associate receives directly from the individual (such as whether and in what time and manner the business associate is to provide the accounting of disclosures to the individual or whether the business associate will forward the request to the covered entity) and the timeframe for the business associate to provide information to the covered entity.]

(h) To the extent the business associate is to carry out one or more of covered entity's obligation(s) under Subpart E of 45 CFR Part 164, comply with the requirements of Subpart E that apply to the covered entity in the performance of such obligation(s); and

(i) Make its internal practices, books, and records available to the Secretary for purposes of determining compliance with the HIPAA Rules.

Permitted Uses and Disclosures by Business Associate

(a) Business associate may only use or disclose protected health information

[Option 1 – Provide a specific list of permissible purposes.]

[Option 2 – Reference an underlying service agreement, such as "as necessary to perform the services set forth in Service Agreement."]

[In addition to other permissible purposes, the parties should specify whether the business associate is authorized to use protected health information to de-identify the information in accordance with 45 CFR 164.514(a)-(c). The parties also may wish to specify the manner in which the business associate will de-identify the information and the permitted uses and disclosures by the business associate of the de-identified information.]

(b) Business associate may use or disclose protected health information as required by law.

(c) Business associate agrees to make uses and disclosures and requests for protected health information

[Option 1] consistent with covered entity's minimum necessary policies and procedures.

[Option 2] subject to the following minimum necessary requirements: [Include specific minimum necessary provisions that are consistent with the covered entity's minimum necessary policies and procedures.]

(d) Business associate may not use or disclose protected health information in a manner that would violate Subpart E of 45 CFR Part 164 if done by covered entity [if the Agreement permits the business associate to use or disclose protected health information for its own management and administration and legal responsibilities or for data aggregation services as set forth in optional provisions (e), (f), or (g) below, then add ", except for the specific uses and disclosures set forth below."]

(e) [Optional] Business associate may use protected health information for the proper management and administration of the business associate or to carry out the legal responsibilities of the business associate.

(f) [Optional] Business associate may disclose protected health information for the proper management and administration of business associate or to carry out the legal responsibilities of the business associate, provided the disclosures are required by law, or business associate obtains reasonable assurances from the person to whom the information is disclosed that the information will remain confidential and used or further disclosed only as required by law or for the purposes for which it was disclosed to the person, and the person notifies business associate of any instances of which it is aware in which the confidentiality of the information has been breached.

(g) [Optional] Business associate may provide data aggregation services relating to the health care operations of the covered entity.

Provisions for Covered Entity to Inform Business Associate of Privacy Practices and Restrictions

(a) [Optional] Covered entity shall notify business associate of any limitation(s) in the notice of privacy practices of covered entity under 45 CFR 164.520, to the extent that such limitation may affect business associate's use or disclosure of protected health information.

(b) [Optional] Covered entity shall notify business associate of any changes in, or revocation of, the permission by an individual to use or disclose his or her protected health information, to the extent that such changes may affect business associate's use or disclosure of protected health information.

(c) [Optional] Covered entity shall notify business associate of any restriction on the use or disclosure of protected health information that covered entity has agreed to or is required to abide by under 45 CFR 164.522, to the extent that such restriction may affect business associate's use or disclosure of protected health information.

Permissible Requests by Covered Entity

[Optional] Covered entity shall not request business associate to use or disclose protected health information in any manner that would not be permissible under Subpart E of 45 CFR Part 164 if done by covered entity. [Include an exception if the business associate will use or disclose protected health information for, and the agreement includes provisions for, data aggregation or management and administration and legal responsibilities of the business associate.]

Term and Termination

(a) <u>Term</u>. The Term of this Agreement shall be effective as of [Insert effective date], and shall terminate on [Insert termination date or event] or on the date covered entity terminates for cause as authorized in paragraph (b) of this Section, whichever is sooner.

(b) <u>Termination for Cause</u>. Business associate authorizes termination of this Agreement by covered entity, if covered entity determines business associate has violated a material term of the Agreement [and business associate has not cured the breach or ended the violation within the time specified by covered entity]. [Bracketed language may be added if the covered entity wishes to provide the business associate with an opportunity to cure a violation or breach of the contract before termination for cause.]

(c) <u>Obligations of Business Associate Upon Termination</u>.

[Option 1 – if the business associate is to return or destroy all protected health information upon termination of the agreement]

Upon termination of this Agreement for any reason, business associate shall return to covered entity [or, if agreed to by covered entity, destroy] all protected health information received from covered entity, or created, maintained, or received by business associate on behalf of covered entity, that the business associate still maintains in any form. Business associate shall retain no copies of the protected health information.

[Option 2 – if the agreement authorizes the business associate to use or disclose protected health information for its own management and administration or to carry out its legal responsibilities and the business associate needs to retain protected health information for such purposes after termination of the agreement]

Upon termination of this Agreement for any reason, business associate, with respect to protected health information received from covered entity, or created, maintained, or received by business associate on behalf of covered entity, shall:

1. Retain only that protected health information which is necessary for business associate to continue its proper management and administration or to carry out its legal responsibilities;

2. Return to covered entity [or, if agreed to by covered entity, destroy] the remaining protected health information that the business associate still maintains in any form;

3. Continue to use appropriate safeguards and comply with Subpart C of 45 CFR Part 164 with respect to electronic protected health information to prevent use or disclosure of the protected health information, other than as provided for in this Section, for as long as business associate retains the protected health information;

4. Not use or disclose the protected health information retained by business associate other than for the purposes for which such protected health information was retained and subject to the same conditions set out at [Insert section number related to paragraphs (e) and (f) above under "Permitted Uses and Disclosures By Business Associate"] which applied prior to termination; and

5. Return to covered entity [or, if agreed to by covered entity, destroy] the protected health information retained by business associate when it is no longer needed by business associate for its proper management and administration or to carry out its legal responsibilities.

[The agreement also could provide that the business associate will transmit the protected health information to another business associate of the covered entity at termination, and/or could add terms regarding a business associate's obligations to obtain or ensure the destruction of protected health information created, received, or maintained by subcontractors.]

(d) Survival. The obligations of business associate under this Section shall survive the termination of this Agreement.

Miscellaneous [Optional]

a. [Optional] Regulatory References. A reference in this Agreement to a section in the HIPAA Rules means the section as in effect or as amended.

b. [Optional] Amendment. The Parties agree to take such action as is necessary to amend this Agreement from time to time as is necessary for compliance with the requirements of the HIPAA Rules and any other applicable law.

c. [Optional] Interpretation. Any ambiguity in this Agreement shall be interpreted to permit compliance with the HIPAA Rules.

Sample Rules of Behavior for Privileged User Accounts

■ **Note** The following statement of understanding and agreement for privileged use is a template that can be adapted for use in your organization and signed by all administrative users of your EMR systems.

The intent of the statement and agreement is to emphasize the fact that the nature of privileged use entails certain abilities to do things in the system that are not advisable or appropriate and which therefore must be governed by a general understanding between administrative security personnel and privileged users.

I adapted the language of this agreement from the United States Department of Health and Human Services agreement for its own administrative users.[1] It is in the public domain and serves as a good starting point for all covered entities in the same area.

---

[1] U.S. Department of Health and Human Services, "Rules of Behavior for Use of HHS Information Resources," July 24, 2013. http://www.hhs.gov/ocio/policy/hhs-rob.html.

Understanding/Agreement of Privileged Use

I understand that as a Privileged User, I must not:

- Share Privileged User account(s) or password(s)/passcode(s)/PIV PINs;

- Install, modify, or remove any system hardware or software without system owner written approval;

- Remove or destroy system audit, security, event, or any other log data;

- Acquire, possess, trade, or use hardware or software tools that could be employed to evaluate, compromise, or bypass information systems security controls;

- Introduce unauthorized code, Trojan horse programs, malicious code, or viruses into HHS information systems or networks;

- Knowingly write, code, compile, store, transmit, or transfer malicious software code, to include viruses, logic bombs, worms, and macro viruses;

- Use Privileged User account(s) for day-to-day communications;

- Elevate the privileges of any user without prior approval from the system owner;

- Use privileged access to circumvent HHS policies or security controls;

- Use a Privileged User account for Web access except in support of administrative related activities; or

- Modify security settings on system hardware or software without the approval of a system administrator and/or a system owner.

I have read the HHS Rules of Behavior for Privileged User Accounts (addendum to the HHS Rules of Behavior (HHS RoB), document number HHS-OCIO-2013-0003S and dated July 24, 2013), and understand and agree to comply with its provisions. I understand that violations of the HHS Rules of Behavior for Privileged User Accounts or information security policies and standards may lead to disciplinary action and that these actions may include termination of employment; removal or disbarment from work on federal contracts or projects; revocation of access to federal information, information systems, and/or facilities; criminal penalties; and/or imprisonment. I understand that exceptions to the HHS Rules of Behavior for Privileged User Accounts must be authorized in advance in writing by the OpDiv Chief Information Officer or his/her designee. I also understand that violation of certain laws, such as the Privacy Act of 1974, copyright law, and 18 USC 2071, which the HHS Rules of Behavior for Privileged User Accounts draw upon, can result in monetary fines and/or criminal charges that may result in imprisonment.

APPROVED BY AND EFFECTIVE ON:

_____   _____

Signed (User)   Date

Breach Notification Process

Note You have secured your organization's data so tight that you won't be susceptible to a breach of unsecured PHI, right? Let's hope that's the case. In the unlikely event that some of that PHI slips out of your control, the following information adapted from the United States Department of Health and Human Services will help you through the process of reporting the breach through the proper channels.[1]

Definition

A *breach* is, generally, an impermissible use or disclosure under the Privacy Rule that compromises the security or privacy of *protected health information* (PHI) such that the use or disclosure poses a significant risk of financial, reputational, or other harm to the affected individual.

---

[1]U.S. Department of Health and Human Services, "Breach Notification Rule," (accessed April 25, 2014). http://www.hhs.gov/ocr/privacy/hipaa/administrative/Breach%20Notification%20Rule/index.html.

The Breach Notification Rule

The Breach Notification Rule requires HIPAA-covered entities to notify individuals and the Secretary of the U.S. Department of Health and Human Services (HHS) of the loss, theft, or certain other impermissible uses or disclosures of unsecured protected health information. In particular, health care providers must promptly notify the Secretary of HHS if there is any breach of unsecured protected health information that affects 500 or more individuals, and notify the media if the breach affects more than 500 residents of a State or jurisdiction. If a breach affects fewer than 500 individuals, the covered entity must notify the Secretary and affected individuals. The covered entity may notify the Secretary of such breaches on an annual basis. Reports of breaches affecting fewer than 500 individuals are due to the Secretary no later than 60 days after the end of the calendar year in which the breaches occurred.

- Significant breaches are investigated by OCR and penalties may be imposed for failure to comply with the HIPAA Rules.

- Breaches that affect 500 or more patients are publicly reported on the OCR website.

- Similar breach notification provisions implemented and enforced by the Federal Trade Commission apply to vendors of personal health records and their third-party service providers.

Your Practice and HIPAA Rules

Who must comply with HIPAA Rules?

"Covered entities" must comply with the HIPAA Privacy and Security Rules:

- Health care providers, including doctors, clinics, hospitals, nursing homes, and pharmacies that electronically transmit any health information in connection with a transaction for which HHS has adopted a standard pursuant to HIPAA administrative simplification, also known as the *transation standard*;

- Health plans; and

- Health care clearinghouses

If you are a covered entity and you have a person or entity that performs certain functions or activities that involve the use or disclosure of protected health information on behalf of, or provides services to, a covered entity, the person or entity is considered a "business associate."

As a covered entity, it is your responsibility to obtain a written contract or agreement that the business associate will appropriately safeguard the PHI created or received on your behalf.

Failure to comply with HIPAA can result in civil and criminal penalties.

Index

A

Access management, 69
  data mapping, 74
  organizational security policy, 75
  periodic access, 74
  role-based access control, 75
    HRIS and medical staff system, 76
    position codes, 76
    RBAC system, 75–77
    rules, 78

Access validation process, 99
  change log, 103
  clinical and rev. cycle, 105
  codes/roles, 105
  formal process, 103
  IT/major build changes, 105
  master schedule, 103
  organization of validation materials, 104
  RBAC system, 106
  sample master schedule, 101
  takeaways, 104
  troubleshooting and support, 106
  validation groupings, 100
  validation session, 101

American Recovery and Reinvestment
    Act (ARRA), 17

B

Broader IT security functions, 149

Build/support team
  application analysts, 39
    analytical, 39
    solution implementer, 40

    successful, 40
    task-oriented, 40

Business associate agreement (BAA), 137
  definitions, 138
  EMR, 138
  payroll, 142
  risk area, 140
    poachers, 140
    teleworkers, 141
  security violation, 139
  targeted view, 139

C, D

Clinical, 38
    chief medical information officer, 38
    director of nursing/nursing
      informatics, 38

CT scan room, 118

E, F, G

Electronic medical record (EMR), 14

Electronic medical record (EMR)
    systems, 1, 63, 133
  application vendors, 3
  arguments, 86
  brass tacks, 83
  break-it analyst, 86
  building blocks, 81
  core skills, 85
  corporate compliance, 134
  E-mail, 135
  emergency department (ED), 87
  features and functions, 90

Electronic medical record (EMR) systems, (*cont.*)
 healthcare providers, 2
 hearts and minds, 136
 herd cats, 3
 HHS website, 66
 HIPAA privacy rule, 88, 91
 holistic approach, 92
 human resources, 134
 implementing and managing, 3
 information security office, 135
 mid-implementation, 5
 mobile devices and patient data, 136
 more-access-is-better analyst, 86
 nonanalyst replacement costs, 84
 organizational goals, 4
 password privacy, 135
 password sharing, 135
 project management office (PMO), 64
 patient data, 2
 post-implementation, 5
 pre-implementation, 5
 removable media, 135
 RN role, 89
 security solutions, 66
 sensitive information, 90
 top–down support, 134

Emergency department (ED), 87

EMR security, 151
 callous or cavalier approach, 154
 plenty of tools, 152
 PMP, 152
 rebaselining, 153
 solid processes, 153
 team, 40

H

Healthcare IT, 9
 budgets, 11
 electronic medical record, 14
 e-mail and file management, 11
 EMR systems, 20
 financial crisis and EMR rush, 17
  ARRA legislation, 17
  HITECH Act, 17
 HITECH Act, 20
 internet connection, downside of, 10

mailroom/facilities management, 11
Medicare and Medicaid, 18
paper transactions
 cost savings, 18
 data sharing process, 9
 information sharing issue, 12–13
 in physician's office, 13
 patient chart, 19
 patient data, 11
Pappalardo's project, 15
 interventions, 16
President Barack Obama, 16
President George W. Bush, 16
privacy violation and identity theft, 19

Health information management, 77

Health Information Technology for
 Economic and Clinical Health Act
 (HITECH Act), 17

Health Insurance Portability and
 Accountability (HIPAA)
privacy and security, 22–23
 accountability, 23
 administrative safeguards, 24
 goals, 29
 HITECH security, 26–27
 minimum necessary, 22
 Omnibus rule of 28, 2013
 Omnibus Rule of 28, 2013
 physical safeguards, 25
 privacy rule, 88
 quality outcomes, 29
 technical safeguards, 25

HITECH Act, 19

Human resources information
 system (HRIS), 71

I, J, K

Identity management, 69
 advantageous, 78
 EHR system, 71
 HL7 interface, 79
 HRIS system, 73
 Identity mapping, 72
 LDAP, 72
 legal medical record (LMR), 79

L

Legal medical record (LMR), 70, 79

Lightweight Directory Access
Protocol (LDAP), 72

M, N

Medical record number (MRN), 125

Microsoft Directory Services
Architecture, 121

MUMPS (Massachusetts General Hospital Utility
Multi-Programming System), 15

O

OSI network model, 79

P, Q

Physical and environmental safeguards, 109
critical/traumatic care areas, 115
EMR implementation, 111
healthcare IT, 110
implement technologies, 114
mitigate risk, 112
olive branches, 113
patient care process, 110
proximity badges/pass codes, 115
public/reception areas, 115

Project Management Institute (PMI), 153

Project management office (PMO), 64, 152

Project Management Professional (PMP), 152

R

Revenue cycle, 38

S

Safeguarding patient data, 123
bigger picture, 127
darned printer, 126
EMR, 125
herding cats/not, 129
medical record number (MRN), 125
nonproduction environments, 128
PHI, 124

Security project/operational support, 143
change control, 149
changes, 147
design, 144
enjoyment, 150
functional groups, 146
integration, 148
post-implementation, 147
reduce, reuse, recycle, 145

Security stakeholders, 41

Security standards, 24
administrative, 24
access controls, 24
accountability, 24
auditing, 24
policies and procedures, 24
physical, 25
technical
authentication, 26
configuration management, 26
data integrity, 25
data protection, 26

Security Workgroup, 41

Stakeholders
health information management
office, 36
HIM analysts, 37
HIM director, 36
information technology
chief security officer, 36
database administrators, 36
help desk/operations staff, 36
security administrators, 36
system administrators, 36
security, 41

Systemwide and client-based
security, 117
EMR, 118–119
directory services integration, 120
et cetera, 120
password age, 120
password length and
complexity, 120
patient data, 121
timeout behavior, 120
hierarchy settings, 118

T, U, V, W

Team, 33
  privacy and security issues, 34
    executive leadership, 35
    physicians, 35
  privacy, compliance and legal, 37
    compliance officer, 37

corporate counsel, 37
  privacy officer, 37
stakeholders, 35
timelines and deliverable dates, 33

X, Y, Z

X-rays, 139

Get the eBook for only $10!

> Now you can take the weightless companion with you anywhere, anytime. Your purchase of this book entitles you to 3 electronic versions for only $10.

This Apress title will prove so indispensible that you'll want to carry it with you everywhere, which is why we are offering the eBook in 3 formats for only $10 if you have already purchased the print book.

Convenient and fully searchable, the PDF version enables you to easily find and copy code—or perform examples by quickly toggling between instructions and applications. The MOBI format is ideal for your Kindle, while the ePUB can be utilized on a variety of mobile devices.

Go to www.apress.com/promo/tendollars to purchase your companion eBook.

Other Apress Business Titles You Will Find Useful

Sensor Technologies
McGrath
978-1-4302-6013-4

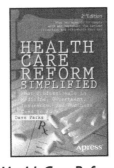

Health Care Reform Simplified, 2nd Edition
Parks
978-1-4302-4896-5

BizTalk 2013 EDI for Health Care
Beckner
978-1-4302-6607-5

Healthcare, Insurance, and You
Zamosky
978-1-4302-4953-5

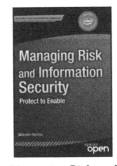

Managing Risk and Information Security
Harkins
978-1-4302-5113-2

The Privacy Engineer's Manifesto
Dennedy/Fox/Finneran
978-1-4302-6355-5

Digital Asset Management
Keathley
978-1-4302-6376-0

Managing Projects in the Real World
McBride
978-1-4302-6511-5

From Techie to Boss
Cromar
978-1-4302-5932-9

Available at www.apress.com